The Healthy Slow Cooker

Ross Dobson

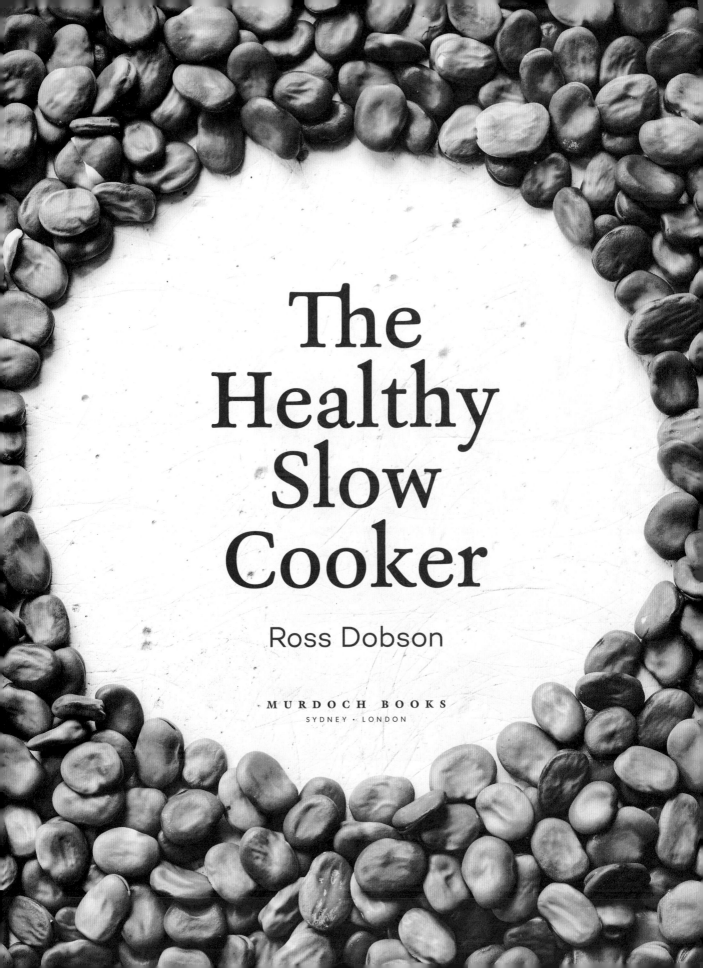

The Healthy Slow Cooker

Ross Dobson

MURDOCH BOOKS
SYDNEY · LONDON

Contents

Slow cooker magic

For many years I ran a busy cafe and restaurant. Year round, the slow cooker would be put to work, quietly simmering away in the background. I'd just throw in a couple of handfuls of dried haricot beans, some mustard, brown sugar and a little smoked pork, and overnight this mixture would magically turn into delicious baked beans in time for breakfast service the next day.

The slow cooker was also the perfect appliance to gently poach chicken, ready to be sliced and served on a bed of spring vegetables and drizzled with a fresh herbaceous dressing. Or it might be used to cook vegetables to perfection in a fragrant tomato base for a Moroccan tagine. When the weather grew chilly, the slow cooker was assigned soup and curry duty, filling the kitchen with fragrant and comforting aromas. And I discovered that a slow cooker was the best way to keep parsnip mash warm, while another one gently simmered beef fillet in red wine, which would later be carved and served on the mash. Time and time again the slow cooker proved itself the most enterprising and time-saving kitchen appliance.

Home-cooked, slow-cooked

At home my slow cooker is rarely used just to keep things warm. Instead, I work with it to make healthy meals that are packed with flavour. And, by 'healthy', I don't mean following a food fad or trend: rather, I like to look to tried-and-true cuisines and flavours, finding inspiration in the freshness of Asian food, with its light broths, clean chilli heat and aromatic herbs and spices. I am also excited by Indian cookery, with its full-throttle flavours and layered spice blends that work so well in a slow cooker. Super-tasty and healthy legumes and pulses combined with fresh vegetables embody the wonderful cuisine of the Middle East – and, when it comes to North African tagines and stews, it really is as if their cooking techniques were made for the slow cooker.

With very little conscious effort on my part much of the food I make in my slow cooker is not only healthy, but it is also often gluten-free, vegan or vegetarian.

The right ingredients

When choosing ingredients, I take a simple and sensible approach. Don't get me wrong – I love a good roast leg of lamb cooked in the oven, where much of the fat can render away and be poured off. However, in the slow cooker, it's different: the fat doesn't escape. So when I do include meat in a recipe, I always trim off excess fat before cooking.

Cheese, especially creamy ricotta and feta, can add richness, but it's umami-packed parmesan that is my favourite and is almost always on hand to finish off a dish. And whatever you do, don't forget about seafood! There's absolutely no reason why fish and seafood shouldn't be at the top of your slow-cooker ingredients list, especially when you want to make something a bit more special. In a slow cooker, the low heat ever so gently poaches and steams seafood to perfection, with little risk of overcooking.

My pantry is full of healthy slow-cooker essentials: canned tomatoes, canned and dried beans and legumes, dried pasta and noodles, good-quality soy sauce and tamari, fish sauce and stock, mustard and cornflour (gluten-free versions of all of these are available). In some recipes I give instructions for making a curry paste, but if you are pressed for time, please feel free to use a ready-made paste – there are some excellent options out there. My fridge is stocked with lots of fresh herbs, vegetables and leafy greens: juicy tomatoes and crisp cucumbers add freshness and crunch; baby spinach, rocket (arugula), shallots and soft herbs like coriander (cilantro) and parsley can be stirred through or scattered over at the end, for a final flourish of flavour and texture.

Choosing your slow cooker

Let's start with the basics: a slow cooker is a kitchen appliance that cooks food over low heat for a long time. A slow cooker has three parts to it. Firstly, there is the actual body of the slow cooker, the heating element or component, along with the electric lead and power controls. Secondly, there is the bowl or pot the food is cooked in, which sits inside the slow cooker. And, finally, we have the lid.

By all means, do some internet research into good brands and models. Just remember that size does matter: you can always use a 6-litre slow cooker to cook a recipe for 2 litres of soup, but not vice versa. Look for a slow cooker with a bowl that is solid and ceramic (which maintains a steady heat better than metal), and with a glass lid so you can actually see what's going on in there. In terms of controls, all you really need are Low and High heat settings (some slow cookers also have a searing option, and one of my slow cookers has an 'Auto' heat setting that I've never used). To keep things simple, the recipes in this book are written with just Low and High heating options. Because I haven't included any recipes for those fatty, dense cuts of meat that require a day's worth of slow cooking, you will find the High setting is used more often than you might expect.

Get off to a good start

Most of the time I turn on the slow cooker as soon as I get going on a recipe. This gives everything a running start. A slow-cooker bowl is generally heavy, thick and ceramic, and a stone-cold bowl will suck the heat from whatever you put in it and prolong the cooking time.

Lifting the lid?

Don't do it! Unless the recipe calls for it, don't be tempted to lift the lid and have a peek. If and when you do take off the lid, you can literally see the heat – in the form of steam – escaping, and this could extend the cooking time by hours. That said, there are quite a few recipes that call for everything to be given a good stir about an hour before the end of the cooking time. But don't worry if you aren't around to do this. After all, one of the great things about a slow cooker is that you can leave the house! No harm will come of just letting it be – and the slow cooker will retain its heat, so when you get home from work or wherever, and the food is cooked, you can turn it off and leave the lid on until you are ready to eat. Just remember to stir thoroughly before serving and scrape down the sides of the bowl (this is often where the tastiest bits are).

It's not all slow ...

There are times when you do need to stir the ingredients in a slow cooker part-way through cooking, and often a recipe will ask you to work quickly after lifting the lid, in order to avoid losing too much heat. So have your spoon at the ready and aim to work quickly!

... but it is all about flavour

When you cook on the stove or in the oven, heat naturally escapes, along with steam, during cooking – and this steady evaporation of water concentrates and intensifies the flavours. But in a slow cooker there is nowhere for this water to go, so it stays right there. Vegetables and even meat can contain surprising amounts of water, potentially making for one big watery bowl of food. To compensate for this, many recipes call for very little additional water, stock or any other liquid. A really good way to boost flavour without adding extra liquid is to use ingredients with a concentrated flavour – think stock powder, soy sauce, fish sauce, salt, pepper and lots of spices. This is one reason why ingredients like these are used so generously in this book. (Another is that they just make everything taste good!)

Good news on the washing-up

You might have come across slow-cooker recipes elsewhere that will have you lightly brush or spray the bowl of the slow cooker with oil prior to cooking – the idea being that it will prevent food from sticking and make the cooker easier to clean. This can be effective if you are cooking fatty meats, whose proteins and fat caramelise and really can make a mess of the bowl, but is not necessary for the lean cuts of meat used in this book – or, of course, for the many non-meat dishes here.

Besides, skipping this step makes for one less thing to do, and the slow-cooker bowl will still have to be cleaned regardless. The easiest way to tackle this is to fill the bowl with warm soapy water and leave it to soak for a few hours, if needed. For stubborn stains, a sprinkling of dishwasher powder added to the water works a treat.

Freezing and reheating

Most ceramic slow-cooker bowls are freezer-proof. Allow the food in the bowl to cool in the fridge first, then remove the lid and cover tightly with plastic wrap before freezing. Thaw in the fridge before returning to the slow cooker. And, of course, never freeze and reheat anything more than once.

Sunday Suppers

Shakshuka

SERVES 4
PREPARATION 15 minutes
COOKING about 3½ hours

1 tablespoon olive oil
1 large red onion, sliced
  into thin wedges
2 cloves garlic, chopped
1 tablespoon sweet paprika
2 teaspoons cumin seeds
400 g (14 oz) can crushed
  tomatoes
400 g (14 oz) can cherry
  tomatoes
1 cup (180 g) sliced roasted
  red capsicum (pepper)
2 tablespoons tomato paste
  (concentrated purée)
4 eggs
large handful flat-leaf
  parsley leaves
large handful mint leaves
toast, to serve

● VEGETARIAN

This one-pot dish is so packed with flavour that it's no surprise it has become such a popular brunch item at cafes. But with this great recipe, there's no reason not to make it at home. Serve with toast to mop up the runny egg yolk and delicious tomato sauce.

Heat your slow cooker to High.

Heat the olive oil in a saucepan over high heat. Add the onion and garlic and fry for a couple of minutes, until the onion is soft. Stir in the paprika and cumin and cook for a minute, until aromatic. Tip in both cans of tomatoes, along with the roasted capsicum and the tomato paste, and stir well. Season generously with salt and pepper, then scrape the whole lot into the bowl of the slow cooker. Cover and cook for 3 hours, until the sauce is thick and bubbling around the edges.

Working quickly to avoid losing too much heat, make four wells in the sauce, each large enough to hold an egg. Crack an egg into a small jug and then pour into a well. Repeat with the other eggs.

Cover and cook for 20–30 minutes, until the egg whites are set but the yolks are still soft (if you want harder yolks, just cook the eggs for a bit longer). Scatter with the herbs and serve with toast on the side.

Asian vegetable, dashi and rice vermicelli hotpot

SERVES 4
PREPARATION 15 minutes
COOKING about 3 hours

100 g (3½ oz) rice vermicelli
    noodles
½ small daikon (white radish)
2 small carrots, sliced
8 fresh shiitake mushrooms
⅓ cup (20 g) dried black
    wood ear mushrooms
8 cups (2 litres) vegetable
    stock
2 tablespoons dashi powder
1 tablespoon gluten-free
    tamari
1 tablespoon white miso
    paste
1 tablespoon mirin
2 loosely packed cups (100 g)
    small kale leaves

● VEGAN
● GLUTEN-FREE

This light and healthy hotpot has a handful of exotic-sounding ingredients, but all are easy to find at Asian supermarkets. Soy sauce and tamari are like non-identical twins: both are made from fermented soy beans and both are packed with umami flavour. The big difference is that tamari is generally, but not always, made without wheat – if you're after gluten-free tamari (and mirin), check the labels carefully before buying.

Put the noodles into a heatproof bowl and pour in enough boiling water to completely cover them. Leave for 10 minutes, until the noodles have softened. Drain well and set aside.

Heat your slow cooker to High.

Peel the daikon and cut in half lengthways. Now cut in half lengthways again and then into slices, to give you rounded triangles. Put these into the bowl of the slow cooker, along with the carrots and both mushrooms.

Combine the stock, dashi, tamari, miso and mirin in a bowl, then pour into the slow cooker. Cover and cook for 2½ hours, until all the vegetables are tender.

Quickly tip the noodles into the slow cooker. No need to stir. Cover and cook for 20–30 minutes, until the noodles are heated through.

Divide the noodles between four serving bowls, then ladle over the broth and vegetables. Scatter with the kale leaves and use chopsticks to stir them into the broth.

Tex Mex black bean and lentil nachos

SERVES 4
PREPARATION 15 minutes
COOKING 2½ hours

400 g (14 oz) can black
  beans
400 g (14 oz) can brown
  lentils
400 g (14 oz) can chopped
  tomatoes
2 tablespoons pickled
  jalapeño slices
1 small red onion, finely
  chopped
2 teaspoons ground cumin
1 teaspoon smoked paprika
½ teaspoon chilli powder
4 handfuls gluten-free
  corn chips
100 g (3½ oz) firm feta,
  finely grated
handful coriander (cilantro)
  leaves

● VEGETARIAN
● GLUTEN-FREE

With a can or two of lentils and beans stored away in the pantry, you'll always be able to conjure up a fuss-free supper. For this Tex Mex-inspired treat, all you need to do is tip everything into the slow cooker and a couple of hours later you're good to go. Spoon over some corn chips for a healthy and very tasty version of nachos, without all the unhealthy paraphernalia that usually accompanies it.

Heat your slow cooker to High.

Tip the beans and lentils into a colander and rinse under the cold tap, using your hands to separate the beans. Drain well, then tip into the bowl of the slow cooker.

Stir in the tomatoes, jalapeños, onion, cumin, paprika and chilli powder. Season generously with salt and pepper, then give everything a good stir to combine. Cover and cook for 2 hours.

Working quickly to avoid losing too much heat, give it a good stir, then cover and cook for 30 minutes.

Meanwhile, preheat the oven to 160°C (315°F) and line a baking tray with baking paper. Scatter over the corn chips, then warm through in the oven for 8–10 minutes.

To serve, spoon the Tex Mex lentils over the warm corn chips and scatter with the feta and coriander.

Chilli beef and bean hotpot

SERVES 4
PREPARATION 20 minutes
COOKING about 4 hours

---

750 g (1 lb 10 oz) lean blade
    steak, cut into large
    bite-sized pieces
2 tablespoons cornflour
400 g (14 oz) can red kidney
    beans, rinsed and well
    drained
400 g (14 oz) can crushed
    tomatoes
½ cup (125 ml) beef stock
2 tablespoons chipotle sauce
2 cloves garlic, crushed
2 teaspoons ground cumin
2 teaspoons smoked paprika
½ teaspoon chilli powder
1 teaspoon ground ginger
handful roughly chopped
    coriander (cilantro)
brown rice, to serve
1 cup (260 g) natural yoghurt,
    to serve

● GLUTEN-FREE

Americans would simply call this 'chili' and would, more often than not, use minced or ground beef. I prefer to choose a specific cut of beef and cut it up myself at home. I am partial to blade steak for this: it keeps its shape even with hours of cooking, yet is still meltingly tender. You don't have to do the cutting yourself, of course - your butcher should be more than happy to oblige.

Heat your slow cooker to High.

Put the beef into a bowl. Sprinkle with the cornflour and a generous seasoning of salt and pepper. Toss the beef to coat well, then tumble into the bowl of your slow cooker. Scatter the beans over the beef.

Tip the tomatoes into the same bowl you used for tossing the beef, then stir in the stock, chipotle sauce, garlic, cumin, paprika, chilli powder and ginger. Pour the lot into the slow cooker, then cover and cook for 2 hours.

Working quickly to avoid losing too much heat, give everything a good stir, then cover and cook for 2 hours, until the beef is very tender.

Stir through the coriander, then serve in bowls with the rice and a dollop of yoghurt.

Paprika chicken hotpot with broken spaghetti

SERVES 4
PREPARATION 20 minutes
COOKING 3½ hours

1 tablespoon extra virgin
    olive oil
400 g (14 oz) can crushed
    tomatoes
½ cup (125ml) chicken stock
2 cloves garlic, chopped
1 red onion, thinly sliced
½ cup (90 g) sliced roasted
    red capsicum (pepper)
2 teaspoons ground cumin
2 teaspoons smoked paprika
handful finely chopped
    flat-leaf parsley
6 chicken thigh fillets
100 g (3½ oz) gluten-free
    spaghetti, roughly broken
4 handfuls baby spinach
    leaves
lemon wedges, to serve

● GLUTEN-FREE

This tasty one-pot meal uses some of my favourite ingredients. Together, the smoky paprika, chicken and lemon create layer upon layer of flavour, all in perfect balance – quite a juggling act!

Heat your slow cooker to High.

In the bowl of your slow cooker, combine the olive oil, tomatoes, stock, garlic, onion, red peppers, cumin, paprika and half of the parsley. Season generously with salt and pepper, then cover and cook for 2 hours to let the flavours develop.

Meanwhile, prepare the chicken by trimming off and discarding the fat. Cut each thigh in half, then refrigerate until needed.

Working quickly to avoid losing too much heat, add the chicken, nudging it into the sauce so it is completely covered. Cover and cook for 1 hour, until the chicken is white and cooked through.

Quickly stir in the pasta, then cover and cook for 30 minutes, until the pasta is tender.

Put a handful of baby spinach leaves into each of four bowls and top with the paprika chicken and pasta. Scatter with the remaining parsley and serve with lemon wedges on the side.

Cauliflower, chickpeas and yoghurt-marinated chicken

SERVES 4
PREPARATION 20 minutes
COOKING 4 hours

1 small head cauliflower,
    preferably with stem
    and leaves intact
400 g (14 oz) can chickpeas,
    rinsed and well drained
2 tablespoons extra virgin
    olive oil
2 tablespoons lemon juice
1 teaspoon fine sea salt
¼ teaspoon ground white
    pepper
½ cup (130 g) natural
    yoghurt
1 teaspoon ground cumin
1 teaspoon garam marsala
1 teaspoon dried methi
    (fenugreek) leaves
2 cloves garlic, finely chopped
3 cm (1¼ in) piece ginger,
    finely grated
8 chicken tenderloins
1 teaspoon smoked paprika
handful flat-leaf parsley
    leaves

● GLUTEN-FREE

This yoghurt marinade is the same one I use for chicken skewers to go on the barbecue, so feel free to give that a try too! Dried methi or fenugreek leaves are my new favourite ingredient: they add a pungent taste and can usually be found at Indian or Middle Eastern shops. Don't feel as though you can't make this without them, however – the dish will be more subtly flavoured, but just as delicious.

Heat your slow cooker to High.

Pull off a few of the outer leaves from the cauliflower and use them to line the base of the slow-cooker bowl.

Cut or break the cauliflower into large florets and arrange in the slow cooker. Scatter in the chickpeas.

In a small bowl, combine the olive oil, lemon juice, sea salt and white pepper, then drizzle over the cauliflower. Cover and cook for 3 hours, until the cauliflower is tender.

While the cauliflower is cooking, combine the yoghurt, cumin, garam marsala, methi leaves, garlic, ginger and a generous seasoning of salt and pepper in a large bowl. Add the chicken and toss to coat in the marinade. Cover and refrigerate for up to 3 hours.

Lay the marinated chicken on top of the cooked cauliflower, scrape in all the yoghurt marinade from the bowl and sprinkle with the paprika. Cover and cook for 1 hour, until the chicken is cooked through.

Transfer everything to bowls, including the cauliflower leaves, and scatter with the parsley.

Caribbean pumpkin, chicken and corn casserole

SERVES 4
PREPARATION 25 minutes
COOKING about 3 hours

1 tablespoon olive oil
1 red onion, thinly sliced
2 cloves garlic, finely chopped
½ teaspoon allspice
1 teaspoon ground ginger
½ teaspoon cayenne pepper
2 tablespoons brown sugar
1 tablespoon Worcestershire
　sauce
1 teaspoon dark soy sauce
400 g (14 oz) can crushed
　tomatoes
¼ cup (60 ml) vegetable
　stock
2 teaspoons cornflour
500 g (1 lb 2 oz) jap pumpkin,
　skin on and cut into
　4–5 cm (1½–2 in) pieces
1 cup (150 g) frozen corn
　kernels
4 chicken thigh fillets
basmati rice, to serve
lime wedges, to serve

Caribbean cooking uses what might seem like an incongruous combination of spices and rather gentrified English ingredients: Worcestershire sauce commonly makes an appearance alongside allspice and cayenne pepper. Dark soy sauce is less traditional, but I often find myself adding just a teaspoon to slow-cooker casseroles to give them an appetisingly rich colour.

Heat your slow cooker to High.

Heat the oil in a frying pan over high heat. Add the onion and garlic and fry for a couple of minutes, just until softened. Stir in the allspice, ginger and cayenne and cook for a minute, until the spices are aromatic. Remove from the heat and stir through the sugar, Worcestershire sauce, soy sauce, tomatoes, stock and cornflour. Tip the whole lot into the bowl of the slow cooker, along with the pumpkin and corn.

Trim off all the fat from the chicken and discard. Cut each thigh in half and add to the slow cooker, nudging the chicken into the sauce. Cover and cook for 2 hours.

Give everything a stir, then quickly cover again to avoid losing too much heat. Cook for 1 hour, until the chicken is cooked through and the pumpkin is tender.

Serve in bowls on a bed of rice, with lime wedges on the side.

Harira

SERVES 4
PREPARATION 20 minutes
COOKING 2½ hours

1 large red onion, finely
chopped
2 cloves garlic, crushed
2 teaspoons ground cumin
2 teaspoons sweet paprika
2 teaspoons ground ginger
½ teaspoon chilli powder
½ teaspoon ground black
pepper
1 stick cinnamon
½ cup (110 g) brown lentils
½ cup (100 g) split red lentils
400 g (14 oz) can chickpeas,
rinsed and well drained
400 g (14 oz) can crushed
tomatoes
2 cups (500 ml) vegetable
stock
1¼ cups (125 g) gluten-free
angel-hair pasta, roughly
broken
½ cup (130 g) natural
yoghurt, to serve
100 g (3½ oz) baby kale
leaves
lemon wedges, to serve
2 tablespoons extra virgin
olive oil

- VEGETARIAN
- GLUTEN-FREE

Traditionally eaten to break the fast during Ramadan, this is a very special Moroccan dish. Often it contains lamb – I haven't included meat here, but do feel free to throw in 300 g (10½ oz) diced lean lamb when you add the lentils and chickpeas, if you like (the cooking time will be the same). This really is one of the most wonderful gluten-free soupy stews you will ever eat. Ditch the yoghurt, and it's vegan too!

Heat your slow cooker to High.

Put the onion, garlic, cumin, paprika, ginger, chilli powder, black pepper, cinnamon, both lentils, chickpeas, tomatoes and stock into the bowl of the slow cooker. Season generously with salt, then give everything a good stir. Cover and cook for 2 hours.

Working quickly to avoid losing too much heat, add the pasta, stirring it into the sauce. Cover and cook for 30 minutes, until the pasta is tender.

Ladle the harira into large bowls. Before serving, top with a dollop of yoghurt and a handful of baby kale leaves, then finish with a squeeze of lemon juice and a drizzle of olive oil.

Black bean ful medames

SERVES 4
PREPARATION 15 minutes
COOKING 3 hours

2 x 400 g (14 oz) cans black
    beans, rinsed and well
    drained
400 g (14 oz) can crushed
    tomatoes
1 tablespoon ground cumin
1 teaspoon chilli powder
1 teaspoon fine sea salt
4 cloves garlic, crushed
large handful flat-leaf
    parsley, finely chopped
4 hard-boiled eggs
handful coriander (cilantro)
    leaves
2 teaspoons toasted sesame
    seeds
1 tablespoon extra virgin
    olive oil

● VEGETARIAN
● GLUTEN-FREE

This ancient recipe is traditionally made with dried fava beans, but I do feel that the black bean lends itself to this beautifully simple dish. After all, the spices used (namely cumin and chilli) are fairly typical of Mexican cookery, which uses black beans in abundance. You'll be amazed at the depth of flavour you can get from such humble ingredients.

Heat your slow cooker to High.

Tumble the beans into the bowl of the slow cooker. Stir through the tomatoes, cumin, chilli powder, salt, garlic, parsley and 1 cup (250 ml) water. Cover and cook for 2 hours.

Give it a stir, then quickly cover again to avoid losing too much heat. Cook for 1 hour, until the sauce is aromatic and has thickened.

Transfer the beans to individual serving bowls. Peel and slice the hard-boiled eggs. Top each serving with slices of egg, scatter with coriander leaves and sesame seeds and drizzle with olive oil.

Sunday chicken dinner

SERVES 4
PREPARATION 20 minutes
COOKING 3 hours

1 parsnip, peeled and cut
   into chunks
4 waxy potatoes, scrubbed
   and sliced lengthways
2 carrots, cut into thin batons
2 cloves garlic, smashed with
   the flat of a knife
1 tablespoon lemon juice
2 tablespoons olive oil
4 small chicken breast fillets
1 cup (140 g) frozen peas
handful finely chopped
   flat-leaf parsley
small handful tarragon leaves

● GLUTEN-FREE

Who would have thought a lean and tasty chicken dinner could all be done in your slow cooker, and with such little effort? My personal preference is to quickly pan-fry the chicken first, to give it a bit of colour. But truth be told, you could skip this step and just lay the well-seasoned chicken breasts directly on the veggies.

Heat your slow cooker to High.

Tumble the parsnip, potatoes, carrots and garlic into the bowl of the slow cooker. Season generously with salt and pepper. Drizzle with the lemon juice and 1 tablespoon of the olive oil. Cover and cook for 2 hours.

Towards the end of the 2 hours, generously season both sides of the chicken fillets with salt and pepper. Heat the remaining olive oil in a large frying pan over high heat. Sear the chicken for 2 minutes each side, just to give it a touch of colour.

Working quickly to avoid losing too much heat, arrange the chicken on top of the root vegetables and scatter in the peas and herbs. Cover and cook for 1 hour, until the chicken is cooked through and the vegetables are tender.

Transfer the chicken and vegetables to plates, then spoon some of the cooking juices over them.

Leg of lamb with oregano, mint and vegetables

SERVES 4
PREPARATION 20 minutes
COOKING about 4 hours

1 tablespoon olive oil
½ leg of lamb, skin removed
1 tablespoon dried oregano
1 tablespoon dried mint
2 teaspoons chilli flakes
8 small waxy potatoes
1 bunch Dutch (baby) carrots,
    trimmed
2 tablespoons lemon juice
1 cup (140 g) frozen peas
large handful green beans,
    ends trimmed
handful finely chopped
    flat-leaf parsley

● GLUTEN-FREE

Here is one of the few instances where I would take the extra time to brown a large piece of meat prior to slow cooking. This does two things: it renders off some of the fat, and also gives the meat an appetising colour. Then all that's left to do is sit the lamb on top of the vegetables and Bob's your uncle!

Heat your slow cooker to High.

Rub the oil all over the lamb and season generously with salt and pepper.

Heat a large frying pan over high heat. When it is smoking hot, add the lamb and cook for 8–10 minutes, turning often, until it is well browned all over. Transfer to a chopping board to cool. When the lamb is cool enough to handle, rub it all over with the oregano, mint and chilli flakes.

Tumble the potatoes and carrots into the bowl of the slow cooker and sit the lamb on top. Pour in the lemon juice, then cover and cook for 3 hours.

Working quickly to avoid losing too much heat, tumble the peas and beans around the lamb. Cover and cook for 1 hour, until the lamb is very tender.

Carefully lift out the lamb and sit it on a chopping board. Use a slotted spoon to transfer the vegetables to a large serving platter. Shred the lamb into large chunks and serve with the veggies. Scatter with the parsley.

Chicken, date and olive tagine

SERVES 4
PREPARATION 15 minutes
COOKING 4 hours

400 g (14 oz) can crushed
    tomatoes
1 tablespoon olive oil
1 large red onion, thinly sliced
2 cloves garlic, crushed
1 teaspoon ground ginger
2 teaspoons ground cumin
2 teaspoons sweet paprika
½ teaspoon ground cinnamon
12 medjool dates
8 chicken tenderloins
½ cup (85 g) large green
    olives
handful chopped coriander
    (cilantro)
handful chopped flat-leaf
    parsley
couscous, to serve

The sweet, aromatic flavours of this tagine typify Moroccan cooking, as does the use of dates or other dried fruit. Ground ginger is a great spice to have on hand. Lacking the fiery heat of fresh ginger, its gentle warmth and earthiness successfully straddle both sweet and savoury cooking.

Heat your slow cooker to High.

Combine the tomatoes, olive oil, onion, garlic, ginger, cumin, paprika and cinnamon in the bowl of the slow cooker. Season generously with salt and pepper, then give everything a good stir. Cover and cook for 2 hours to let the flavours develop.

Stir through the dates, then cover and cook for 1 hour.

Working quickly to avoid losing too much heat, add the chicken to the slow cooker, nudging it into the sauce so it is completely covered. Cover and cook for 1 hour, until the chicken is white and cooked through.

Stir in the olives and herbs, then serve with couscous.

Indian spiced root vegetables

SERVES 4
PREPARATION 20 minutes
COOKING about 4 hours

---

1 tablespoon olive oil

1 red onion, thinly sliced

2 cloves garlic, finely chopped

2 cm (¾ in) piece ginger,
    finely chopped

1 teaspoon ground cumin

½ teaspoon chilli flakes

3 tablespoons chicken or
    vegetable stock

4 small waxy potatoes,
    halved

200 g (7 oz) pumpkin, skin on
    and cut into wedges

2 small parsnips, peeled and
    quartered

4 hard-boiled eggs

handful mint leaves

handful flat-leaf parsley
    leaves

lime wedges, to serve

● GLUTEN-FREE

Rather like an exotic bubble and squeak, but starting with raw veggies and giving them an Indian twist, there's no need to wait until you have leftovers from a roast dinner to give this a try. As well as being a comforting supper, it makes an awesome brunch, topped with your favourite style of egg. I can never get enough boiled eggs, and I'm particularly partial to a roughly chopped hard-boiled egg.

Heat your slow cooker to High.

Heat the olive oil in a frying pan over high heat. Add the onion, garlic and ginger and stir-fry for 2–3 minutes, until aromatic. Stir through the cumin and chilli and season generously with salt and pepper. Stir in the stock, then remove from the heat.

Tumble the potatoes, pumpkin and parsnips into the bowl of the slow cooker.

Pour the stock mixture over the vegetables, then cover and cook for 3 hours. Give everything a gentle stir, so you don't break up the veggies too much, then cover and cook for 1 hour, until the vegetables are tender. Taste for seasoning, adding more salt if you like.

Transfer to a serving platter. Peel and roughly chop the hard-boiled eggs, then scatter over the vegetables, along with the herbs. Serve with lime wedges on the side.

Soy bean, chicken and carrot casserole with chilli oil

SERVES 4
PREPARATION 15 minutes
SOAKING overnight
COOKING about 5½ hours

½ cup (95 g) dried soy beans
6 Dutch (baby) carrots,
    roughly chopped
3 cups (750 ml) chicken stock
1 tablespoon light soy sauce
2 teaspoons white miso paste
½ teaspoon sesame oil
2 tablespoons mirin
2 tablespoons cornflour
8 chicken tenderloins
steamed jasmine rice,
    to serve
1 large red chilli, seeded
    and thinly sliced
small handful coriander
    (cilantro) leaves
chilli oil, to serve

Soy beans have a fresh, nutty flavour that goes so well with the delicate chicken, savoury miso and sweet mirin in this hearty, clean-tasting casserole. Canned, ready-to-go soy beans are often tricky to find, so I've used dried here – just remember that they will need an overnight soaking in cold water beforehand.

Soak the soy beans in cold water overnight. Next day, drain and discard the water. Put the soy beans into a saucepan and cover with cold water. Bring to the boil over high heat and cook for 30 minutes, topping up the water as needed.

Meanwhile, heat your slow cooker to High.

Drain the beans, then tip into the bowl of the slow cooker and add the carrots.

Combine the stock, soy sauce, miso, sesame oil and mirin in a bowl or jug, giving it a good stir to break up the miso, then pour into the slow cooker. Cover and cook for 3 hours.

In a small bowl, mix the cornflour with 2 tablespoons water to make a smooth paste. Stir into the slow cooker, then add the chicken, nudging it into the sauce so it is completely covered. Reduce the heat to Low, then cover and cook for 2 hours, until the chicken is white and cooked through and the soy beans are tender.

Serve in bowls on a bed of jasmine rice. Scatter with the chilli and coriander, and serve the chilli oil alongside for drizzling.

Weekday Dinners

Chicken 'shawarma'

SERVES 4–6
PREPARATION 20 minutes
COOKING about 3 hours

8 chicken thigh fillets
2 tablespoons olive oil
2 brown onions, sliced into
   wedges
3 cloves garlic, roughly
   chopped
1 tablespoon ground cumin
1 tablespoon ground
   coriander
2 teaspoons sweet paprika
1 teaspoon ground ginger
1 teaspoon ground turmeric
1 teaspoon ground cinnamon
¼ teaspoon ground cloves
2 bay leaves
¾ cup (200 g) natural
   yoghurt
2 tablespoons lemon juice
2 tomatoes, sliced, to serve
1 small red onion, thinly
   sliced, to serve
handful coriander (cilantro)
   leaves, to serve
handful mint leaves, to serve
6 small wholemeal flatbreads,
   to serve

Although this is by no means a traditional shawarma, where the meat is spit-roasted, the luscious, spiced sauce renders the chicken melt-in-your-mouth tender and delicious. Roll into flatbread wraps with tomato, onion and herbs – or serve with rice for a perfectly acceptable gluten-free version.

Heat your slow cooker to High.

Trim the chicken of excess fat and discard. Cut each thigh in half, then refrigerate until needed.

Heat the olive oil in a frying pan on high heat. Add the brown onions and cook for 4–5 minutes, stirring to separate the slices, until they are turning golden. Add the garlic, cumin, coriander, paprika, ginger, turmeric, cinnamon, cloves and bay leaves and cook for a minute, until the spices are fragrant. Add 2 tablespoons water and stir to remove any stuck-on bits. Remove from the heat, stir through the yoghurt and lemon juice, then scrape the lot into the bowl of the slow cooker.

Add the chicken thighs to the sauce, nudging them down so they are mostly submerged. Cover and cook for 2 hours.

Give it a stir, then quickly cover again to avoid losing too much heat. Cook for 1 hour, until the chicken is very tender and easily falls apart. Use a slotted spoon to transfer the chicken to a serving dish, then spoon over some of the sauce.

Serve with the tomatoes, red onion, fresh herbs and flatbread, letting people make up their own wraps.

Lemony lentil, potato and chickpea stew

SERVES 2 as a main
or 4 as a side
PREPARATION 15 minutes
COOKING 3 hours

8 waxy potatoes, skin on and
halved lengthways
1 cup (215 g) green lentils
400 g (14 oz) can chickpeas,
rinsed and well drained
2 tablespoons finely chopped
preserved lemon
1 cup (250 ml) vegetable
stock
1 tablespoon extra virgin
olive oil
¼ cup (60 ml) lemon juice
1 teaspoon cumin seeds
1 teaspoon dried mint
small handful finely chopped
fresh mint
small handful finely chopped
flat-leaf parsley, plus extra
leaves, to serve
100 g (3½ oz) ricotta salata
or pecorino, shaved

● VEGETARIAN
● GLUTEN-FREE

I would really urge you to seek out a waxy variety of potato for this. It's not just about them holding their shape – you need a potato that has enough texture and bite to go up against the robust chickpeas. This makes a lovely lunch or supper as is, but I can never resist serving a bit of grilled steak or fish alongside.

Heat your slow cooker to High.

Tumble the potatoes, lentils and chickpeas into the bowl of the slow cooker. Season generously with salt and pepper.

In a small bowl, combine the preserved lemon, stock, olive oil, lemon juice, cumin seeds, dried and fresh mint and the finely chopped parsley. Pour into the slow cooker, then cover and cook for 2 hours.

Turn the slow cooker down to Low and cook for 1 hour, until the potatoes are cooked through.

Serve on a large platter, garnished with the extra parsley leaves and the shaved cheese.

Chicken puttanesca with gnocchi

SERVES 4
PREPARATION 15 minutes
COOKING about 3½ hours

1 tablespoon extra virgin
olive oil
1 red onion, thinly sliced
2 cloves garlic, finely chopped
small handful flat-leaf
parsley, finely chopped
1 teaspoon dried oregano
½ cup (125 ml) red wine
400 g (14 oz) can crushed
tomatoes
1 tablespoon small capers,
rinsed and drained
2 anchovy fillets, chopped
2 tablespoons tomato paste
(concentrated purée)
1 tablespoon cornflour
6 large chicken thigh fillets
300 g (10½ oz) gluten-free
gnocchi, to serve
50 g (1¾ oz) parmesan

● GLUTEN-FREE

Some people shriek in horror at the mere suggestion of an anchovy. True, they are not the most attractive looking or smelling ingredient, but when cooked down into a sauce they virtually disappear, imparting a complex savoury flavour. All the other ingredients here have the sunny disposition of the Mediterranean and perfectly complement the tender chicken.

Heat your slow cooker to High.

In the bowl of the slow cooker, combine the olive oil, onion, garlic, parsley, oregano, red wine, tomatoes, capers, anchovies, tomato paste, cornflour and ¼ cup (60 ml) water. Season generously with salt and pepper. Give it a good stir to make sure the cornflour has completely dissolved.

Trim the chicken thighs of excess fat and discard. Cut each thigh in half, then add to the slow cooker, nudging them into the sauce so they are completely submerged. Cover and cook for 2 hours, until the sauce is bubbling around the edges.

Give everything a stir, then quickly cover again to avoid losing too much heat. Cook for 1 hour, until the chicken is tender and cooked through.

Tumble the gnocchi into the slow cooker, gently nudging them into the sauce and around the chicken (avoid stirring as this will allow too much heat to escape). Cover and cook for 20–30 minutes, until the gnocchi is done.

Transfer the chicken and gnocchi to serving bowls and grate the parmesan over the top.

Greek-style octopus

SERVES 4
PREPARATION 20 minutes
COOKING about 4 hours

1 cup (250 ml) white wine vinegar

1 kg (2 lb 4 oz) octopus, cleaned

1 tablespoon extra virgin olive oil

400 g (14 oz) can crushed tomatoes

¼ cup (60 ml) red wine

1 tablespoon tomato paste (concentrated purée)

4 cloves garlic, roughly chopped

2 bay leaves

2 cloves

1 stick cinnamon

handful roughly chopped dill

handful finely chopped flat-leaf parsley

4 waxy potatoes, thickly sliced

12 cherry tomatoes

● GLUTEN-FREE

There are many tricks to tenderising octopus prior to cooking. I thought I'd heard it all until I discovered that, on a commercial scale, this is often done by tumbling the octopus with some smooth pebbles in a small cement mixer. Don't worry, though, no cement mixers are needed here! A young Greek guy at my local fish market explained to me how his family readies octopus for slow cooking – simply blanch for 5 minutes in water and vinegar. It's too easy and very effective.

To blanch the octopus, combine 4 litres water and the vinegar in a large saucepan. Bring to the boil. Add the octopus, cover the pan and cook for 5 minutes. Drain the octopus in a colander, shaking off as much water as possible. Transfer to a plate and, when the octopus is cool enough to handle, cut each octopus into four (two tentacles apiece), then set aside.

Heat your slow cooker to High.

In the bowl of the slow cooker, combine the olive oil, crushed tomatoes, red wine, tomato paste, garlic, bay leaves, cloves, cinnamon, dill, parsley and a generous seasoning of salt and pepper. Add the potatoes, cherry tomatoes and octopus, nudging them all into the sauce. Cover and cook for 4 hours, until the sauce is bubbling around the edges and the octopus is very tender.

Serve in bowls.

Mujadara

SERVES 4
PREPARATION 15 minutes
COOKING about 1½ hours

1 tablespoon olive oil
1 teaspoon cumin seeds
2 bay leaves
6 dried chillies
1½ cups (300 g) basmati rice
¼ cup (55 g) green lentils
2½ cups (625 ml) vegetable
    stock
handful flat-leaf parsley
    leaves
1 tablespoon lime juice
gluten-free flatbread,
    to serve
natural yoghurt, to serve

● VEGETARIAN
● GLUTEN-FREE

Originating from the Middle East, this earthy dish of spiced rice and lentils really lends itself to slow cooking. The spices are first warmed in a little oil to bring out their flavour before being cooked with the rice and lentils. Basmati rice has nutty, long grains that stay firm; avoid using other varieties here, or the rice will absorb too much liquid and become gluggy.

Heat your slow cooker to High.

Heat the olive oil in a frying pan over medium heat. When the oil is hot, add the cumin seeds, bay leaves and dried chillies and stir for a moment or two, just until aromatic. Tip into the bowl of the slow cooker.

Put the rice and lentils into a colander and give them a quick rinse under the cold tap. Shake dry, then tip them into the slow cooker. Add the stock and a generous seasoning of salt and pepper, then give everything a good stir. Cover and cook for 1½ hours, until the liquid has been absorbed by the rice and lentils.

Transfer to a large platter, scatter with the parsley and drizzle with the lime juice. Serve with flatbread and yoghurt.

Ginger and black bean chicken with green veggies

SERVES 4
PREPARATION 15 minutes
COOKING 2 hours

8 chicken tenderloins
2 spring onions (scallions),
    thinly sliced
3 cm (1¼ in) piece ginger,
    thinly sliced
3 cloves garlic, finely chopped
2 tablespoons Chinese black
    beans, roughly chopped
1 teaspoon sesame oil
3 tablespoons Chinese
    rice wine
1 teaspoon brown sugar
2 teaspoons cornflour
1 green capsicum (pepper),
    thinly sliced
1 bunch broccolini, separated
    into individual stems
1 zucchini (courgette), cut
    into thick rounds
large handful Thai basil
    leaves

● GLUTEN-FREE

Chinese black beans aren't actually black beans at all, but fermented soy beans. Here these funky little beans impart savoury umami flavours to beautifully tender chicken. Stating the obvious, they are the main ingredient in the Chinese black bean sauce you see in supermarkets. But do try and find the unadulterated ingredient from a good Asian grocer and let your black bean addiction begin! You only need to use a few to get a good flavour boost and they will keep for ages.

Heat your slow cooker to High.

In a bowl large enough to hold the chicken, combine the spring onions, ginger, garlic, black beans, sesame oil, rice wine, brown sugar and cornflour. Add the chicken and toss to coat, then tumble the lot into the bowl of the slow cooker. Cover and cook for 1½ hours, until the sauce is bubbling around the edges and the chicken is white and cooked through.

Give everything a quick stir, then arrange the capsicum, broccolini and zucchini on top of the chicken to steam. Cover and cook for a further 30 minutes, until the vegetables are cooked but still crisp.

Transfer the vegetables to a bowl. Serve the chicken on plates with the vegetables on the side. Garnish with Thai basil.

Pork, sweet potato and pear stew

SERVES 4
PREPARATION 25 minutes
COOKING 3 hours

1 small sweet potato, skin on,
   cut into semi-circles
4 lean pork leg steaks, about
   150–175 g (5½–6 oz) each
2 bosc or other firm pears,
   each cut into 8 pieces
4 cloves garlic, smashed with
   the flat of a knife
1½ cups (375 ml) chicken
   stock
2 tablespoons maple syrup
1 tablespoon cornflour
1 teaspoon dark soy sauce
¼ teaspoon ground black
   pepper
handful finely chopped
   flat-leaf parsley

Pork can be a tricky meat to use in a slow cooker, especially if you are looking for a healthy recipe. Not all pork is fatty, though. Just choose a lean cut and trim off any visible fat before you start. Cooked to melting tenderness, this pork is so good, with notes of musky sweetness from the pear and sweet potato. A firm variety of pear, such as bosc, will keep its shape better.

Heat your slow cooker to High.

Tip the sweet potato into the slow cooker. Trim off any fat from the pork and discard, then lay the pork on top of the sweet potato. Tumble the pears and garlic over the pork.

In a bowl or jug, combine the stock, maple syrup, cornflour, soy sauce and black pepper, stirring to dissolve the cornflour, then pour into the slow cooker. Cover and cook for 3 hours, until the pork and vegetables are tender.

Use a slotted spoon to transfer the sweet potato, pork and pears to a serving platter. Pour some of the sauce over the top and scatter with the parsley.

Turmeric beef stew

SERVES 6
PREPARATION 25 minutes
COOKING 4 hours

2 brown onions, peeled
1 kg (2 lb 4 oz) chuck steak
2 tablespoons cornflour
2 cups (500 ml) beef stock
1 teaspoon fish sauce
1 tablespoon ground turmeric
1 tablespoon ground cumin
½ teaspoon chilli powder
1 large tomato, roughly
    chopped
handful roughly chopped
    coriander (cilantro)
¼ cup (35 g) roasted
    peanuts, roughly chopped
basmati rice, to serve

● GLUTEN-FREE

The texture of the beef in this recipe is as sublime as the deep golden hue of the turmeric-infused sauce. And while a tablespoon of turmeric might sound like a lot, I promise you it works a treat. This is one of those unassuming sorts of recipes that you cook and eat, and then just wonder where all the deliciousness comes from.

Heat your slow cooker to High.

Cut the onions in half from stem to root end, then lay cut side down on a chopping board and cut, again from stem to root end, into thin wedges. Tumble the onions into the bowl of the slow cooker, using your hands to separate the layers of onion.

Trim off all the fat from the steak and discard. Cut the steak into 4–5 cm (1½–2 in) chunks. Put into a bowl, sprinkle with the cornflour and toss to coat well. Arrange the meat in a single layer on top of the onions in the slow cooker.

In the same bowl you used to toss the beef, combine the stock, fish sauce, turmeric, cumin, chilli powder and a generous grinding of black pepper. Give it a good stir to incorporate any remaining cornflour stuck to the bowl, then pour into the slow cooker. Add the tomato, then cover and cook for 2 hours.

Give everything a stir, then quickly cover again to avoid losing too much heat. Cook for a further 2 hours, until the meat is tender and clothed in a rich turmeric-coloured gravy.

Transfer to a large serving bowl and scatter with the coriander and peanuts.

Serve with basmati rice.

Vietnamese beef stew

SERVES 4
PREPARATION 20 minutes
COOKING about 3¼ hours

750 g (1 lb 10 oz) blade steak
2 tablespoons oyster sauce
1 teaspoon dark soy sauce
2 teaspoons sesame oil
1 brown onion, thinly sliced
3 cloves garlic, roughly
    chopped
2 cups (500 ml) beef stock
¼ teaspoon freshly ground
    black pepper
1 tablespoon cornflour
2 stalks lemongrass, white
    parts only, cut into 5 cm
    (2 in) lengths
3 star anise
3 cinnamon sticks
2 ripe tomatoes, cut into
    wedges
100 g (3½ oz) rice vermicelli
    noodles
large handful Vietnamese
    mint leaves
large handful coriander
    (cilantro) leaves

● GLUTEN-FREE

This one takes its cue from the wonderful aromatic flavours that define Vietnamese food: lemongrass, star anise and cinnamon make for a fresh and fragrant one-pot meal. An added bonus is the inclusion of silky rice vermicelli noodles.

Heat your slow cooker to High.

Trim all the fat off the beef and discard. Cut the beef into 4–5 cm (1½–2 in) chunks. Add the meat to the bowl of the slow cooker, along with the oyster sauce, soy sauce, sesame oil, onion, garlic, stock, black pepper and cornflour. Give everything a good stir, making sure the cornflour has dissolved. Scatter the lemongrass, star anise and cinnamon over the stew, then cover and cook for 2 hours.

Give it a gentle stir, nudging the star anise and cinnamon into the sauce, then quickly cover again to avoid losing too much heat. Cook for 1 hour, until the beef is aromatic and tender. Tumble the tomato wedges into the slow cooker, then cover again and turn down to Low.

Put the noodles into a heatproof bowl and pour in enough boiling water to cover. Leave for 10 minutes, until softened. Drain well.

Gently stir the noodles into the slow cooker, then transfer the beef stew, noodles and all, to four bowls. Pour in the aromatic broth and scatter with the herbs.

Veal meatballs with spinach and chickpeas

SERVES 4
PREPARATION 30 minutes
COOKING about 2 hours

1 tablespoon extra virgin
   olive oil
1 small brown onion, finely
   chopped
2 cloves garlic, finely chopped
½ teaspoon chilli flakes
¼ teaspoon ground mace
   or nutmeg
400 g (14 oz) can crushed
   tomatoes
handful roughly chopped dill
handful roughly chopped
   flat-leaf parsley
400 g (14 oz) can chickpeas,
   rinsed and well drained
2 large handfuls baby spinach
   leaves
finely grated pecorino,
   to serve

MEATBALLS
750 g (1 lb 10 oz) veal mince
½ cup (30 g) fresh wholemeal
   breadcrumbs
2 spring onions (scallions),
   thinly sliced
2 cloves garlic, finely chopped
1 teaspoon fennel seeds,
   roughly chopped
2 tablespoons finely grated
   pecorino

Few things are as comforting as a meatball. And the first time you do them in the slow cooker will have you asking why you haven't tried it before. The sauce can be made in advance, well in advance if you so wish. The two golden rules of slow cooking must be adhered to for this: don't lift the lid, and don't stir too much. You want the heat to stay in the slow cooker, not escape!

Heat your slow cooker to High.

Heat the olive oil in a frying pan over medium heat. Add the onion and garlic and fry for just a couple of minutes, to soften without browning. Scrape into the bowl of the slow cooker, then add the chilli flakes, mace, tomatoes, dill, parsley, chickpeas and a good seasoning of salt and pepper. Give everything a good stir to combine. Cover and leave to cook while you make the meatballs.

For the meatballs, put the mince, breadcrumbs, spring onions, garlic, fennel seeds, pecorino and a generous seasoning of salt and pepper into a bowl. Use your hands to squeeze the mixture together until it is really well combined. Wet your hands and form the mixture into walnut-sized balls.

Drop the meatballs into the slow cooker, cover and cook for 2 hours, until cooked through. Stir through the spinach, then cover and cook for a few minutes, just until it has wilted.

Transfer to serving plates and scatter with grated pecorino.

Bolognese with big pasta

SERVES 4
PREPARATION 15 minutes
COOKING about 2 hours

1 tablespoon olive oil
1 onion, finely chopped
3 cloves garlic, finely chopped
1 small carrot, finely chopped
1 stalk celery, finely chopped
500 g (1 lb 2 oz) beef mince
1 teaspoon dried oregano
1 bay leaf
400 g (14 oz) can crushed
    tomatoes
250 g (9 oz) cherry tomatoes
3 cups (750 ml) tomato
    passata (puréed tomatoes)
1 cup (80 g) rigatoni
    or other large pasta
finely grated parmesan,
    to serve

I really like cooking pasta in my slow cooker, not least because it means less equipment and less washing up. The only trick – and this is a good thing for the carb-conscious – is not to add too much pasta. A cup or so will do nicely.

Heat your slow cooker to High.

Put the olive oil into a large frying pan and set over high heat. Add the onion, garlic, carrot and celery and cook for just a couple of minutes, until the onion has softened a little. Stir through the mince, oregano and bay leaf and fry for a few minutes, until the meat is brown. Stir through the canned and cherry tomatoes and the passata.

Pour half of the meat sauce into the bowl of the slow cooker. Scatter in the pasta, keeping it away from the edges, and pour on the rest of the sauce. Cover and cook for 2 hours, until the sauce is bubbling and the pasta is tender.

Serve in bowls, with a grating of parmesan on top.

Lamb and rhubarb khoresh

SERVES 4
PREPARATION 20 minutes
COOKING 3½ hours

---

4 lean lamb leg steaks,
    about 600 g (1 lb 5 oz)
    in total
3 stalks rhubarb, cut into
    2–3 cm (¾–1¼ in) pieces
400 g (14 oz) can cherry
    tomatoes
handful finely chopped
    flat-leaf parsley
4 green cardamom pods,
    lightly smashed
½ teaspoon ground turmeric
2 teaspoons dried mint
3 cm (1¼ in) piece ginger,
    coarsely grated
2 cloves garlic, finely chopped
large pinch saffron strands
1 red onion, thinly sliced
1 cup (250 ml) chicken stock
handful mint leaves, to serve

● GLUTEN-FREE

Khoresh is an exotic-sounding Iranian term for a stew, where a whole bunch of ingredients are gently cooked together in a pot to produce a delicious meal. For this one, I've made things even more exotic by including rhubarb, which is more often cooked with lots of sugar. But as a savoury ingredient, rhubarb is tangy and sour, with a citrusy tang that marries beautifully with the other Persian flavours here.

Heat your slow cooker to High.

Trim off all the fat from the lamb and discard. Cut each steak into three or four and put into the bowl of the slow cooker.

Set aside a third of the rhubarb. Tumble the remaining rhubarb over the lamb and season generously with salt and pepper.

In a bowl, combine the tomatoes, parsley, cardamom, turmeric, dried mint, ginger, garlic, saffron, onion and stock, then tip the lot into the slow cooker. Cover and cook for 2 hours.

Give it a gentle stir, trying not to break up the rhubarb too much, then quickly cover again and cook for 1 hour.

Tumble the reserved rhubarb into the slow cooker, then cover and cook for 30 minutes, until it is just tender.

Serve the khoresh in small bowls, garnished with mint leaves.

Mussels in tomato and fennel broth with pearl couscous

SERVES 2 as a main
or 4 as a starter
PREPARATION 15 minutes
COOKING 3½ hours

400 g (14 oz) can crushed
    tomatoes
¼ cup (60 ml) fish stock
¼ cup (60 ml) white wine
3 small or baby fennel bulbs,
    thinly sliced, feathery tops
    reserved
2 cloves garlic, finely chopped
small handful roughly
    chopped flat-leaf parsley
1 tablespoon olive oil
⅓ cup (70 g) pearl or Israeli
    couscous
1 kg (2 lb 4 oz) ready-to-cook
    black mussels
lemon wedges, to serve

All those mussel shells take up a lot of space in your slow cooker, and so this recipe will only serve two people as a meal. That said, it also makes a really lovely starter for four. With mussels, the secret is not to overcook them – but many myths prevail. They do not have to be cooked so long that their shells are wide open, revealing shrivelled and embarrassed-looking mussels. As soon as the shells start to pop open, they are ready.

Heat your slow cooker to High.

Combine the tomatoes, stock, wine, sliced fennel, garlic, parsley, olive oil and a generous seasoning of salt and pepper in the bowl of the slow cooker. Cover and cook for 2½ hours, until the fennel is very tender.

Stir the couscous into the tomato and fennel broth. Cover and cook for 30 minutes, until the couscous has doubled in size. Add the mussels and give the slow cooker a gentle shake, so the mussels settle into the broth. Cover and cook for a further 30 minutes, until the mussels have just opened.

Transfer to a large serving bowl, discarding any unopened mussels. Scatter with the reserved fennel tops and serve with lemon wedges on the side.

Lemongrass chicken

SERVES 4
PREPARATION 20 minutes
COOKING 2¼ hours

2 large chicken breast fillets
1 small bunch coriander
　　(cilantro), with roots
2 tablespoons oyster sauce
2 teaspoons sesame oil
2 teaspoons fish sauce
1 tablespoon brown sugar
1 stalk lemongrass, white part
　　only, thinly sliced
3 cloves garlic, finely chopped
3 cm (1¼ in) piece galangal,
　　peeled and coarsely grated
½ teaspoon freshly ground
　　black pepper
1 leek, white part only,
　　thinly sliced
1 red capsicum (pepper),
　　cut into thin strips
1 zucchini (courgette),
　　cut into chunks
basmati rice, to serve

● GLUTEN-FREE

While this may look like a light, lean meal, it is not light on flavour. The fast and fresh tastes of Asia are right at home in a slow cooker, and are used here in abundance. Don't stress if you can't get your hands on galangal; ginger can be used in its place - and both can be sliced, chopped or grated and then frozen, ready for when you next need them.

Heat your slow cooker to High.

Cut the chicken into 4–5 cm (1½–2 in) chunks and place in the bowl of the slow cooker.

Pick the leaves off the coriander and set them aside for later. Scrape the roots clean and wash well to remove any dirt. Finely chop the roots and stems, then scatter over the chicken. Add the oyster sauce, sesame oil, fish sauce, sugar, lemongrass, garlic, ginger and black pepper to the slow cooker. Use your hands or tongs to toss everything around until well combined.

Cover and cook for 1½ hours, until the sauce is bubbling around the edges and the chicken is white and cooked through. Give everything a good stir, then tumble in the leek, capsicum and zucchini. Cover and cook for 45 minutes, until the vegetables are tender but still crisp.

Serve the chicken, vegetables and sauce on a bed of basmati rice, garnished with the reserved coriander leaves.

Potato and green bean sambal

SERVES 4
PREPARATION 20 minutes
COOKING 3 hours

400 g (14 oz) can crushed
tomatoes
2 large red chillies, roughly
chopped
2 cloves garlic, roughly
chopped
2 cm (¾ in) piece ginger,
roughly chopped
1 tablespoon fish sauce
2 tablespoons brown sugar
3–4 coriander (cilantro) roots,
scraped clean and well
washed
8 baby potatoes, quartered
150 g (5½ oz) green beans,
trimmed and halved
lengthways
1 small head broccoli,
trimmed and broken
into small pieces
brown rice, to serve
lemon wedges, to serve

● GLUTEN-FREE

In Bali, a warung is a small family-run eating house that sells simple, home-cooked food. Generally speaking, the dishes are wonderfully tasty and healthy, often with a chilli-hot sambal base to them. If you make this recipe and are a fan, feel free to mix it up a bit by adding sweet potato or pumpkin.

Heat your slow cooker to High.

Put the tomatoes, chillies, garlic, ginger, fish sauce, sugar and coriander roots into the bowl of a food processor and process until smooth. Tip into the bowl of the slow cooker. Stir in the potatoes and beans, then cover and cook for 2 hours.

Stir through the broccoli. Cover and cook for 1 hour, until all the vegetables are tender.

Serve on a bed of brown rice, with lemon wedges on the side.

Set and
Forget

Mexican three-bean and tomato burritos

SERVES 6
PREPARATION 20 minutes
COOKING 6 hours

400 g (14 oz) can red kidney
    beans
400 g (14 oz) can butter
    beans
400 g (14 oz) can black
    beans
400 g (14 oz) can cherry
    tomatoes
½ cup (90 g) sliced roasted
    red capsicum (pepper)
1 small red onion, thinly sliced
1 clove garlic, crushed
2 teaspoons chicken stock
    powder
1 tablespoon ground cumin
½ teaspoon chilli powder
½ iceberg lettuce, shredded
gluten-free flatbreads
    or tortillas
2 avocados, diced
large handful coriander
    (cilantro) leaves
lime wedges, to serve

● GLUTEN-FREE

This has zing and freshness written all over it. I'm also thinking this combination would make for great nachos: simply substitute the flatbread with gluten-free corn chips and maybe even scatter with some crumbled feta cheese. For an even more fuss-free version of this, simply serve in bowls with corn chips on the side and a big dollop of light sour cream or yoghurt on top.

Heat your slow cooker to Low.

Tip all the beans into a large colander and rinse under cold water, using your hands to separate the beans. Drain well and tip the beans into the bowl of the slow cooker.

Add the tomatoes, capsicum, onion, garlic, stock powder, cumin and chilli powder to the beans and season generously with salt and pepper. Give everything a good stir to combine. Cover and cook for 6 hours, until the mixture is aromatic and the beans are thickly coated in the sauce.

Transfer to a serving bowl.

Scatter some lettuce over each flatbread and top with the beans, avocado and coriander leaves. Serve with lime wedges on the side.

Chicken, apricot and pumpkin stew

SERVES 4
PREPARATION 15 minutes
COOKING 6 hours

8 chicken thigh fillets
1 cup (250 ml) chicken stock
6 fresh apricots, halved and
  stoned
200 g (7 oz) jap pumpkin,
  skin on, cut into wedges
1 small red onion, finely
  chopped
2 cloves garlic, finely chopped
2 teaspoons ground cumin
2 teaspoons sweet paprika
½ teaspoon chilli flakes
1 tablespoon cornflour
1 bay leaf
handful finely chopped
  flat-leaf parsley
handful coriander (cilantro)
  leaves

● GLUTEN-FREE

Some of us grew up with something called 'apricot chicken', a recipe in which chicken is cooked with packet French onion soup and canned apricot nectar. Thankfully, the recipe here lacks the hefty salt and sugar content of its forebear. What's more, a vegan version can easily be made by substituting the chicken with 500 g (1 lb 2 oz) peeled and chopped sweet potato, although the cooking time might need to be increased slightly. In a slow cooker, vegetables like sweet potatoes and carrots often take longer to cook than you might think.

Heat your slow cooker to Low.

Remove excess fat from the chicken fillets and discard. Cut each fillet into three pieces. Put the chicken in the bowl of the slow cooker, together with the stock, apricots, pumpkin, onion, garlic, cumin, paprika, chilli flakes, cornflour, bay leaf, parsley and a generous seasoning of salt and pepper. Give it all a good stir to combine. Cover and cook for 6 hours.

Before serving, stir gently, being careful not to break up the pumpkin, which will be very tender. Add salt and pepper to taste, if needed, then transfer to serving plates and garnish with coriander leaves.

Fragrant lamb and orzo casserole

SERVES 4
PREPARATION 15 minutes
COOKING 9 hours

400 g (14 oz) lamb leg steaks
400 g (14 oz) can crushed
    tomatoes
2 tablespoons tomato paste
    (concentrated purée)
½ cup (125 ml) beef stock
1 stick cinnamon
2 bay leaves
2 cloves
1 teaspoon dried oregano
handful finely chopped
    flat-leaf parsley
½ cup (125 g) orzo or risoni
½ cup (about 30 g) crumbled
    kefalograviera cheese
handful small basil
    or marjoram leaves
lemon wedges, to serve

Greek cooking is so much more than feta and olives. Cinnamon, bay leaves and cloves add spicy warmth to this rich and hearty casserole. Kefalograviera is a hard, salty sheep's cheese that can be tricky to find, but I've made this many times with shavings of parmesan or pecorino and they work nicely too. The casserole can be left to cook all day while you are at work, then all you need to do when you get home is stir through the pasta and dinner will be ready in an hour!

Heat your slow cooker to Low.

Trim off any fat from the lamb and discard. Cut each lamb steak in half.

Combine the tomatoes, tomato paste, stock, cinnamon, bay leaves, cloves, oregano and parsley in the bowl of the slow cooker. Generously season with salt and pepper and give everything a good stir. Add the lamb, nudging it into the sauce, then cover and cook for 8 hours.

Stir through the orzo, cover and cook for 1 hour, until the lamb is very tender and the orzo is cooked.

Serve the casserole in bowls, scattered with the cheese and basil or marjoram leaves, and with lemon wedges on the side.

Smoky chipotle baked beans

SERVES 4
PREPARATION 10 minutes
SOAKING overnight
COOKING 8–10 hours

1 cup (200 g) dried haricot
    beans
400 g (14 oz) can chopped
    tomatoes
2 tablespoons chipotle sauce
1 tablespoon smoked paprika
1 tablespoon mild mustard
2 tablespoons maple syrup
    or date syrup
1 tablespoon brown sugar
sliced wholemeal bread,
    toasted
handful micro-kale or cress

● **VEGAN**

Although baked beans are often thought of as a breakfast or brunch item, they're also great as a TV-and-chill type of meal. Haricot beans are sometimes confused with their slightly larger cousin, the great northern white bean. But for proper baked beans, haricots are hard to beat: they're the traditional bean for Boston baked beans and they're also the cute little bean used in your everyday can of baked beans. Don't forget the dried beans need to be soaked overnight before you start, though.

Soak the beans in a bowl of cold water overnight.

Next day, heat your slow cooker to Low.

Drain the beans and tip them into the bowl of the slow cooker. Add the tomatoes, chipotle sauce, paprika, mustard, maple or date syrup, brown sugar and 2 cups (500 ml) water. Season generously with salt and pepper, then give everything a good stir to combine.

Cover and cook for 8–10 hours, until the beans have just about doubled in size and are tender.

Stir thoroughly, then serve the beans on toast, topped with a sprinkling of micro-kale or cress.

Turkish green beans with tomato

SERVES 4
PREPARATION 20 minutes
COOKING 6 hours

400 g (14 oz) can crushed tomatoes
2 tablespoons tomato paste (concentrated purée)
1 cup (180 g) sliced roasted red capsicum (pepper)
2 tablespoons date syrup
1 tablespoon ground cumin
1 tablespoon sweet paprika
1 tablespoon olive oil
1 red onion, sliced
2 cloves garlic, crushed
750 g (1 lb 10 oz) green beans
1 cup (220 g) ready-made hummus, to serve
gluten-free pita bread, to serve

- VEGAN
- GLUTEN-FREE

In this classic Middle Eastern recipe, green beans are slowly cooked, rendering them beautifully tender and sweetly spiced. And being vegan and gluten-free, it will keep everyone happy. The date syrup adds richness and a hint of sweetness; it can be found at Middle Eastern food shops and some supermarkets, but you could substitute molasses or honey at a pinch.

Heat your slow cooker to Low.

Add the crushed tomatoes, tomato paste, roasted capsicum, date syrup, cumin, paprika, olive oil, red onion, garlic and a generous seasoning of salt and pepper to the bowl of the slow cooker. Give everything a good stir to combine.

Trim any woody stems off the beans and discard. Tumble the beans into the slow cooker, nudging them into the sauce. Cover and cook for 6 hours, until the sauce is hot and bubbling around the edges.

Give everything a good stir, making sure you scrape down the sides of the bowl – this is where the flavour is. Have a taste and add more salt and pepper if needed, then serve with hummus and pita bread on the side.

Turkey with rosemary, tomatoes and feta

SERVES 4
PREPARATION 25 minutes
COOKING 3 hours

1 red onion, thinly sliced
2 cloves garlic, finely chopped
1 small stem rosemary
2 bay leaves
handful finely chopped
    flat-leaf parsley
4 small waxy potatoes, cut
    into bite-sized pieces
750 g (1 lb 10 oz) turkey
    breast fillet
1 tablespoon cornflour
400 g (14 oz) can cherry
    tomatoes
1½ cups (375 ml) chicken
    stock
1 tablespoon extra virgin
    olive oil
2 large handfuls baby rocket
    (arugula)
150 g (5½ oz) feta, crumbled
lemon wedges, to serve

● GLUTEN-FREE

I'm a fan of turkey: it is a meat that is both lean and full of flavour. And I'm disappointed that – except for the few weeks prior to Christmas – it is not nearly as available as I'd like. The good news is that chicken breast fillet can most definitely be used instead of turkey here.

Heat your slow cooker to High.

Place the onion, garlic, rosemary, bay leaves, parsley and potatoes in the bowl of the slow cooker. Season generously with salt and pepper and toss to combine.

Cut the turkey into large bite-sized pieces and put into a bowl. Sprinkle with the cornflour and a generous seasoning of salt and pepper, then toss to coat. Tip the turkey into the slow cooker, along with the tomatoes and stock, then drizzle with the olive oil. Cover and cook for 3 hours, until the turkey is cooked through and the potatoes are tender.

Transfer to a large serving dish and scatter with the rocket and feta. Serve with lemon wedges on the side.

Tender beef with sweet potato and aromatic spices

SERVES 6
PREPARATION 15 minutes
COOKING 8½ hours

2 small brown onions, thinly sliced
4 cloves garlic, roughly chopped
3 cm (1¼ in) piece ginger, roughly chopped
1 tablespoon ground cumin
1 tablespoon sweet paprika
4 black cardamom pods, lightly crushed
½ cup (85 g) raisins
400 g (14 oz) can diced tomatoes
1 tablespoon olive oil
1 kg (2 lb 4 oz) chuck or gravy beef
1 tablespoon cornflour
1 cup (250 ml) chicken stock
200 g (7 oz) sweet potato, cut into large chunks
large handful roughly chopped coriander (cilantro)
brown basmati rice, to serve

● GLUTEN-FREE

This aromatic melange of sweet spices and raisins complements tender beef beautifully. Chuck steak is my all-time favourite cut for slow cooking, but gravy beef or blade make good substitutes.

Heat your slow cooker to Low.

Put the onions, garlic, ginger, cumin, paprika, cardamom, raisins and tomatoes in the bowl of your slow cooker. Season generously with salt and pepper, then give everything a good stir. Drizzle the olive oil over the top.

Trim any visible fat off the beef and discard. Cut the beef into 3–4 cm (1¼–1½ in) chunks and put into a bowl. Sprinkle with the cornflour, then toss to coat. Tumble the beef into the slow cooker, nudging it into the tomato mixture. Pour in the stock. Place the sweet potato on top of the beef, then cover and cook for 8 hours.

Working quickly to avoid losing too much heat, give everything a good stir, making sure you scrape the sides of the bowl. Cover and cook for 30 minutes – just enough time to cook the rice, ready to be served alongside.

Transfer to a serving bowl, scatter with the coriander and serve with the rice.

Beef, sweet potato and date tagine

SERVES 4
PREPARATION 20 minutes
COOKING 8 hours

750 g (1 lb 10 oz) blade steak
2 teaspoons ground cumin
2 teaspoons sweet paprika
1 teaspoon ground ginger
1 tablespoon cornflour
2 red onions, sliced
1 small sweet potato, peeled
    and cut into thick rounds
12 medjool dates
2 x 400 g (14 oz) cans whole
    tomatoes, drained
2 tablespoons date syrup
handful small coriander
    (cilantro) leaves
handful small mint leaves

● **GLUTEN-FREE**

I sometimes feel like a broken record espousing the virtues of Moroccan cooking in slow cookers – but its flavours and techniques really are perfectly suited to them. For this tagine, everything is literally just thrown into the slow cooker and time does the rest, making this an ideal dish to put together before you head out of the door in the morning.

Heat your slow cooker to Low.

Trim off all the fat from the beef and discard. Cut the beef into large bite-sized pieces and put into a bowl. Add the cumin, paprika, ginger, cornflour and a generous seasoning of salt and pepper. Toss to coat the beef, then tumble into the bowl of the slow cooker. Cover the beef with the onions, followed by the sweet potato and dates.

In the same bowl you used for tossing the beef, combine the tomatoes and date syrup. Roughly mash the tomatoes with a potato masher or fork, then tip into the slow cooker. Cover and cook for 8 hours, until everything is tender and aromatic.

Stir gently, then transfer to bowls and scatter with the herbs.

Smoky bean, corn and chicken hotpot

SERVES 4
PREPARATION 25 minutes
COOKING 6 hours

4 chicken thigh fillets
400 g (14 oz) can black
   beans
400 g (14 oz) can black-eyed
   beans
400 g (14 oz) can crushed
   tomatoes
1 small red onion, thinly sliced
2 cloves garlic, finely chopped
2 teaspoons smoked paprika
2 teaspoons ground cumin
½ teaspoon chilli powder
2 corn cobs, each cut
   into 4 pieces
½ cup (125 ml) chicken stock
1 teaspoon cornflour
1 tablespoon extra virgin
   olive oil
½ cup (50 g) finely grated
   parmesan

● GLUTEN-FREE

This recipe is a hearty amalgam of nutty and nourishing beans, corn and my absolute favourite slow-cooker meat, chicken thighs. A final sprinkling of parmesan adds extra punch.

Heat your slow cooker to Low.

Trim off all the fat from the chicken and discard. Cut each thigh in half.

Tip both beans into a colander and rinse under the cold tap, using your hands to separate the beans. Drain well, then tip into the bowl of the slow cooker. Add the tomatoes, onion, garlic, paprika, cumin, chilli powder and a generous seasoning of salt and pepper. Give it a good stir to combine.

Tumble the corn pieces into the slow cooker, then sit the chicken in between them, nudging both corn and chicken into the bean mixture.

In a small bowl, mix the stock and cornflour until smooth. Stir into the slow cooker, then drizzle in the olive oil. Cover and cook for 6 hours.

Give everything a good stir, separating any ingredients that are stuck together, and making sure you stir through any tasty bits from the sides of the bowl.

Transfer to a large serving dish and scatter with parmesan.

Broccoli with chilli, lemon and ricotta

SERVES 4
PREPARATION 5 minutes
COOKING 3 hours

1 large head broccoli,
  with stem intact
2 large red chillies, seeded
  and thinly sliced
2 cloves garlic, finely chopped
½ teaspoon fennel seeds
½ teaspoon chilli flakes
¼ cup (60 ml) extra virgin
  olive oil
¼ cup (60 ml) vegetable
  stock
2 cups (460 g) low-fat ricotta
2 tablespoons lemon juice
handful flat-leaf parsley
  leaves
lemon wedges, to serve

● VEGETARIAN
● GLUTEN-FREE

Broccoli may look like a fragile vegetable that belongs only in a quickly cooked stir-fry or pasta sauce, but in fact it can stand up to hours of cooking. During this time, the most delicious part of the broccoli, the hard stem, is rendered soft and tender. When you cut broccoli for the slow cooker, do so lengthways, keeping the stem intact – this will hold the whole thing together.

Heat your slow cooker to High.

Cut the broccoli into large florets, leaving the stem intact to prevent the broccoli from falling apart as it cooks.

Arrange the broccoli in the bowl of the slow cooker.

Scatter in the red chilli, garlic, fennel seeds and chilli flakes. Season generously with salt and pepper, then pour in the olive oil and stock. Cover and cook for 3 hours, until the broccoli is fork-tender.

Spread the ricotta onto a large serving platter, making wells that will catch the cooking juices. Spoon the broccoli onto the ricotta using a slotted spoon, then pour some of the cooking juices over the top. Drizzle with the lemon juice, scatter with parsley leaves and serve with lemon wedges on the side.

Lamb with white beans, tomato and jalapeños

SERVES 4
PREPARATION 15 minutes
COOKING 8 hours

750 g (1 lb 10 oz) lean lamb
1 brown onion, finely chopped
4 cloves garlic, finely chopped
400 g (14 oz) can crushed
    tomatoes
2 tablespoons pickled
    jalapeños, plus 1 tablespoon
    brine from the jar
handful finely chopped
    flat-leaf parsley
2 teaspoons ground cumin
400 g (14 oz) can white
    beans, rinsed and well
    drained
1 tablespoon extra virgin
    olive oil

● GLUTEN-FREE

This has a couple of the things you want from a good recipe covered: it requires very little effort on your part, and there are relatively few ingredients. The lamb and beans are simply slow cooked in a rich tomato sauce flavoured with pickled jalapeños, which add a spicy heat and clean tanginess. A jar of these is a great thing to have lurking in the back of the fridge.

Heat your slow cooker to Low.

Trim off any excess fat from the lamb and discard. Cut the meat into large bite-sized pieces, then put into the bowl of the slow cooker. Scatter in the onion and garlic.

In a bowl, combine the tomatoes, jalapeños and brine, parsley, cumin and beans and season generously with salt and pepper. Tip the lot into the slow cooker, then drizzle with the olive oil. Cover and cook for 8 hours.

Give everything a good stir, making sure you scrape down the sides of the bowl, then transfer to a serving dish.

Poached salmon with verjuice, potatoes, chilli and herbs

SERVES 4
PREPARATION 15 minutes
COOKING 6½ hours

1 tablespoon verjuice
1 tablespoon extra virgin
   olive oil
1 large red chilli, thinly sliced
2 spring onions (scallions),
   thinly sliced at an angle
12 baby potatoes
large handful mint leaves,
   thinly sliced
handful flat-leaf parsley,
   finely chopped
handful dill, finely chopped
4 salmon fillets, about
   150–175 g (5½–6 oz) each,
   skinned and pin-boned
lemon wedges, to serve

● **GLUTEN-FREE**

Verjuice is the juice of unripe grapes, and it brings a delicious sweet-and-sour note to these elegant, omega-rich salmon fillets. The fish is simply steamed in the slow cooker once the potatoes are done, and the whole lot is bathed in fresh-tasting cooking juices spiked with chilli and herbs.

Heat your slow cooker to Low.

In a large bowl, combine the verjuice, olive oil, chilli, spring onions, potatoes and herbs. Season generously with salt and pepper, then toss together and tip the lot into the bowl of the slow cooker. Cover and cook for 6 hours.

Working quickly to avoid losing too much heat, give it a quick stir, then lay the salmon on top of the potatoes. Cover and cook for 30 minutes, until the salmon is pale pink and can be easily flaked with a fork.

Use a slotted spoon to transfer the potatoes and salmon to a large serving platter. Spoon some of the cooking juices over the top and serve with lemon wedges.

Cajun spiced bean medley

SERVES 4
PREPARATION 25 minutes
COOKING 6 hours

2 x 400 g (14 oz) cans
    four-bean mix, rinsed
    and well drained
400 g (14 oz) can crushed
    tomatoes
½ cup (125 ml) vegetable
    stock
1 teaspoon cornflour
1 red onion, finely chopped
1 stalk celery, finely chopped
½ cup (90 g) sliced roasted
    red capsicum (pepper)
2 cloves garlic, finely chopped
6 sprigs thyme
3 bay leaves
handful finely chopped
    flat-leaf parsley
2 teaspoons ground cumin
2 teaspoons sweet paprika,
    plus extra for sprinkling
½ teaspoon chilli powder
1 tablespoon snipped chives
1 cup (245 g) light sour cream
gluten-free corn chips,
    to serve

● VEGETARIAN
● GLUTEN-FREE

There is something rather special about the humble canned four-bean mix. Often it comes to the rescue in a last-minute salad for a barbecue, but here the beans are combined with a swag of Cajun flavours to make a sensational meal. Served up with corn chips and sour cream, it's bordering on indulgent.

Heat your slow cooker to Low.

Tip the beans into the bowl of the slow cooker. Add the tomatoes, stock, cornflour, onion, celery, capsicum, garlic, thyme, bay leaves, parsley, cumin, paprika and chilli powder. Season generously with salt and pepper, then give everything a good stir. Cover and cook for 6 hours, until the beans are soft and the sauce is thick.

Give everything a good stir, making sure you scrape down the sides of the bowl to incorporate all the tasty bits.

Have a taste and add more salt and pepper if needed, then transfer to a serving bowl and scatter with the snipped chives. Serve the sour cream in a bowl on the side, sprinkled with the extra paprika. Eat with gluten-free corn chips.

Soups

Souk-style chicken and chickpea soup

SERVES 4
PREPARATION 15 minutes
COOKING 3 hours

1 tablespoon olive oil
2 cloves garlic, finely chopped
1 small red onion, finely
     chopped
400 g (14 oz) can crushed
     tomatoes
400 g (14 oz) can chickpeas,
     rinsed and well drained
3 cups (750 ml) chicken stock
1 carrot, finely chopped
1 stalk celery, with leaves,
     finely chopped
1 teaspoon ground cumin
1 teaspoon sweet paprika
1 teaspoon ground ginger
¼ teaspoon ground turmeric
½ teaspoon ras el hanout
2 chicken breast fillets
small handful flat-leaf
     parsley leaves
small handful mint leaves
extra virgin olive oil, to serve

● GLUTEN-FREE

In the souks of Marrakesh, stallholders arrange their vibrantly coloured, aromatic spices in conical shapes, somewhat like the lid of a tagine, to entice customers to buy. Inspired by these bustling markets, this soup uses spices that are typical of Moroccan cooking, with the added bonus that they're all available at your local supermarket.

Heat your slow cooker to High.

Put the olive oil, garlic, onion, tomatoes, chickpeas, stock, carrot, celery, cumin, paprika, ginger, turmeric and ras el hanout in the bowl of the slow cooker. Generously season with salt and pepper and give everything a good stir to combine. Cover and cook for 2 hours.

Immerse the chicken breast fillets in the soup. Cover and cook for 1 hour, until the chicken is white and just cooked through. Remove the chicken to a chopping board. Turn the slow cooker down to Low and leave covered.

When the chicken is cool enough to handle, use two forks or your fingers to roughly shred the meat into strands. Return the chicken to the slow cooker and stir to combine.

Serve the soup in bowls, scattered with parsley and mint leaves and drizzled with olive oil.

Hot-and-sour noodle soup

SERVES 4
PREPARATION 10 minutes
COOKING 2¼ hours

¼ cup (60 ml) light soy sauce
½ cup (125 ml) Chinese black vinegar or rice vinegar
6 dried red chillies
3 cm (1¼ in) piece ginger, thinly sliced
225 g (8 oz) can sliced bamboo shoots, well drained
200 g (7 oz) shiitake mushrooms, larger ones halved
200 g (7 oz) small button mushrooms
2 spring onions (scallions), white parts only, thinly sliced
½ teaspoon freshly ground black pepper
½ teaspoon ground white pepper
8 cups (2 litres) vegetable stock
2 ripe tomatoes, cut into wedges
100 g (3½ oz) enoki mushrooms
300 g (10½ oz) semi-firm tofu, cubed
2 tablespoons cornflour
200 g (7 oz) fresh udon noodles

● VEGAN

With a perfect balance of sour tang from the black vinegar and bite from the pepper, this Chinese soup is incredibly tasty. Such full-on flavours are mildly tempered by the soothing vegetables and tofu, while the noodles add substance and texture.

Heat your slow cooker to High.

Put the soy sauce, vinegar, dried chillies, ginger, bamboo shoots, shiitake and button mushrooms, spring onions, black and white pepper, and all except ½ cup (125 ml) of the stock into the bowl of the slow cooker. Cover and cook for 1 hour to allow the flavours to develop.

Stir through the tomatoes, enoki mushrooms and tofu, then cover and cook for 1 hour.

In a small bowl or jug, mix the cornflour into the remaining stock until smooth, then stir into the soup. Stir through the noodles, then quickly cover again to avoid losing too much heat. Cook for a further 15 minutes, until the soup has thickened slightly and the noodles are hot.

Serve in large bowls.

Pea and sweet potato soup with shredded chicken

SERVES 4
PREPARATION 25 minutes
COOKING about 4 hours

8 cups (2 litres) vegetable
   stock
1 small brown onion, finely
   chopped
2 cloves garlic, finely chopped
1½ cups (235 g) fresh or
   frozen garden peas
1 small white-fleshed sweet
   potato, cut into bite-sized
   chunks
1 carrot, finely chopped
4 small potatoes, quartered
1 teaspoon dried mint
2 small chicken breast fillets
handful mint leaves
zest of 1 lemon

● GLUTEN-FREE

Do try and source fresh peas for this. During the lengthy cooking the peas will lose their vibrancy, but not their sweetness. I love poaching chicken in my slow cooker: it only needs about an hour and then it is ready for a quick shredding before being returned to the soup.

Heat your slow cooker to High.

Combine the stock, onion, garlic, peas, sweet potato, carrot, potatoes and dried mint in the bowl of the slow cooker. Cover and cook for 3 hours, until all the vegetables are tender.

Working quickly to avoid losing too much heat, add the chicken to the slow cooker, nudging it into the soup so it is completely covered. Cover and cook for 1 hour, until the chicken is white and cooked through.

Transfer the chicken to a plate or chopping board. Turn the slow cooker down to Low and leave the soup covered to keep warm.

When the chicken is cool enough to handle, use your fingers or two forks to shred the meat into strips. Stir the chicken back into the soup.

Serve in bowls, garnished with mint leaves and lemon zest.

Chicken and rice soup with lettuce and lemon

SERVES 4
PREPARATION 20 minutes
COOKING about 3 hours

8 skinless chicken drumsticks
6 cups (1.5 litres) chicken stock
1 tablespoon gluten-free tamari
2 tablespoons lemon juice
1 clove garlic, crushed
3 cm (1¼ in) piece ginger, finely grated
¼ cup (50 g) jasmine rice
½ head iceberg lettuce, shredded
small handful finely chopped coriander (cilantro)
lemon wedges, sesame oil and white pepper, to serve

● GLUTEN-FREE

Lettuce is often stir-fried in Chinese cooking and lends itself nicely to the slow cooker, where it cooks to a silky tenderness. The finished soup is sort of like a congee, the much-loved Chinese rice porridge, with a similar cleansing simplicity.

Heat your slow cooker to High.

Arrange the chicken in the bowl of the slow cooker. Add the stock, tamari, lemon juice, garlic and ginger, then scatter in the rice. Give it a gentle stir to submerge the rice in the stock. Cover and cook for 2½ hours.

Use a slotted spoon to transfer the chicken to a plate. Keep the slow cooker covered while the chicken cools. When it is cool enough to handle, shred all the meat from the bones and discard the bones. Put the meat back into the slow cooker, along with the lettuce and coriander. Cover and cook for 30 minutes, until the lettuce has wilted.

Serve the soup in large bowls with lemon wedges on the side. Finish with sesame oil, to taste, and a little white pepper.

Black-eyed bean, brown rice and silverbeet soup

SERVES 4
PREPARATION 15 minutes
SOAKING overnight
COOKING 6 hours

1 cup (185 g) dried black-eyed beans
½ cup (100 g) brown basmati rice
4 cups (1 litre) vegetable stock
400 g (14 oz) can crushed tomatoes
1 leek, white part only, thinly sliced
1 stalk celery, finely chopped
handful roughly chopped flat-leaf parsley
2 tablespoons extra virgin olive oil
4 large silverbeet leaves

● VEGAN
● GLUTEN-FREE

When in season, silverbeet is as cheap as the proverbial chip, and it can pretty much be used in place of any other greens in this book that are to be cooked. Here it shines in a wholesome and earthy black-eyed bean soup.

Soak the beans in a bowl of cold water overnight.

Next day, heat your slow cooker to High.

Put the drained black-eyed beans, rice, stock, tomatoes, leek, celery, half of the parsley and half of the olive oil into the bowl of the slow cooker. Season generously with salt and pepper, then give everything a good stir. Cover and cook for 4 hours.

Remove the thick white stems of the silverbeet and discard. Finely shred the leaves and add to the slow cooker. Cover and cook for 2 hours, until the beans are tender and the silverbeet is very soft.

Serve the soup in large bowls, scattered with the remaining parsley and drizzled with the remaining olive oil.

Tuscan kale, white bean and lemon soup

SERVES 4
PREPARATION 15 minutes
COOKING 3 hours

6 cups (1.5 litres) vegetable stock
1 small brown onion, finely chopped
1 stalk celery, finely chopped
2 cloves garlic, finely chopped
⅓ cup (65 g) basmati rice
400 g (14 oz) can white beans, rinsed and well drained
2 bunches Tuscan kale, finely chopped
¼ cup (60 ml) lemon juice
small handful finely chopped flat-leaf parsley
1 tablespoon extra virgin olive oil
¼ cup (25 g) finely grated parmesan

● VEGETARIAN
● GLUTEN-FREE

We may think of kale as a trendy new ingredient, but it's been around for ages – centuries, in fact. Tuscan kale, aka cavolo nero, has a long history in Italian cuisine and has a multitude of uses, but to my mind is really made for soups. With hours of cooking, the crinkly leaves will stay firm and sweet as it turns almost inky-black ('nero' is Italian for black).

Heat your slow cooker to High.

Combine the stock, onion, celery, garlic and rice in the bowl of the slow cooker. Cover and cook for 2 hours, until the rice and vegetables are tender.

Stir through the white beans and kale, then cover and cook for 1 hour, until the kale is wilted and tender.

Stir through the lemon juice and parsley, then transfer to a serving dish. Drizzle with the olive oil and sprinkle with the parmesan. Ladle into serving bowls.

Red lentil, pumpkin and lime pickle soup

SERVES 4
PREPARATION 20 minutes
COOKING about 4 hours

1½ cups (305 g) split red
    lentils
6 cups (1.5 litres) salt-
    reduced vegetable stock
2 tablespoons chopped
    Indian lime pickle
500 g (1 lb 2 oz) pumpkin,
    peeled, seeded and
    cut into cubes
1 tablespoon olive oil
1 red onion, finely chopped
1 teaspoon cumin seeds
1 large tomato, finely
    chopped
handful mint leaves
handful dill sprigs

● VEGAN
● GLUTEN-FREE

Lime (or mango) pickle is one of the tastiest things to have on hand. Not only is it a spicy and sweet condiment to serve with curries, it's pretty good with crackers and cheddar too! And a few tablespoons of chopped lime pickle stirred through a soup really make it dance with zesty flavour.

Heat your slow cooker to High.

Combine the lentils, stock and lime pickle in the bowl of the slow cooker. Cover and cook for 2 hours.

Working quickly to avoid losing too much heat, stir through the pumpkin and season generously with salt. Cover and cook for a further 2 hours, until both the lentils and pumpkin are soft. Turn the slow cooker down to Low and keep covered.

Heat the olive oil in a small saucepan over high heat. Add the onion and cook for 8–10 minutes, until golden. Stir in the cumin seeds and cook for 1 minute, until the cumin pops and sizzles. Tip the spicy onions into the soup and stir through, along with the chopped tomato. Add pepper to taste – and a little more salt, if needed.

Serve the soup in small bowls, garnished with the herbs.

Chicken dumpling soup with Asian vegetables and noodles

SERVES 4
PREPARATION 30 minutes
COOKING 4 hours

6 cups (1.5 litres) chicken
    stock
1 tablespoon soy sauce
    or tamari
1 tablespoon mirin
2 stalks celery, thinly sliced
¼ Chinese cabbage, chopped
1 small bunch Chinese
    broccoli
200 g (7 oz) fresh Chinese
    thin egg noodles
1 spring onion (scallion),
    extra-thinly sliced
    at an angle, to garnish
sesame oil, to serve

CHICKEN DUMPLINGS
500 g (1 lb 2 oz) chicken
    mince
1 spring onion (scallion),
    thinly sliced
2 canned water chestnuts,
    drained and finely chopped
1 tablespoon finely grated
    ginger
1 tablespoon cornflour
2 teaspoons nori seaweed
    flakes
1 teaspoon soy sauce
    or tamari

This soup is so full of healthy verdant colour and umami flavour. I like to make the dumpling mixture beforehand and keep it in the fridge, but you could easily swap things around and get your soup going first, then mix, roll and dunk the dumplings. There is something magical about drizzling sesame oil into a hot soup.

To make the dumplings, put the chicken mince, spring onion, water chestnuts, ginger, cornflour, seaweed flakes and tamari into a bowl and mix until thoroughly combined. Cover and refrigerate until needed.

Heat your slow cooker to High.

Combine the stock, tamari, mirin, celery and cabbage in the bowl of the slow cooker. Trim the tough ends off the Chinese broccoli and discard. Pull apart the leaves and stems, but leave them whole. Toss into the slow cooker, then give everything a good stir. Cover and cook for 1½ hours, until the stock is hot and the vegetables have wilted. Leave the slow cooker covered while you shape the dumplings.

Wet your hands with water and roll the chicken mixture into balls about the size of a walnut. When all the dumplings are formed, drop them into the hot broth in the slow cooker. Cover and cook for 2 hours, until they are cooked through.

In a colander, rinse the noodles with boiling water to remove excess starch. Drain well, then tip into the slow cooker. Cover and cook for 30 minutes, until the noodles are cooked.

Transfer to large serving bowls. Scatter over the thinly sliced spring onion and drizzle with sesame oil.

Mushroom, buckwheat and leek soup

SERVES 4
PREPARATION 10 minutes
COOKING about 4 hours

8 cups (2 litres) vegetable
  stock
1 cup (195 g) buckwheat
2 carrots, finely chopped
2 stalks celery, finely chopped
2 cloves garlic, crushed
small handful finely chopped
  flat-leaf parsley
1 tablespoon olive oil
1 leek, thinly sliced
2 cups (180 g) roughly
  chopped open-cap
  mushrooms
2 cups (180 g) roughly
  chopped button
  mushrooms
2 cups (180 g) thinly sliced
  Swiss brown mushrooms

● VEGAN
● GLUTEN-FREE

Given time, leeks will cook down to silky softness. This also brings out their natural sweetness, which explains why they make such a lovely addition to pies, stews and just about any soup you can think of. Here mushrooms create an umami-packed broth and buckwheat brings nutty wholesomeness.

Heat your slow cooker to High.

Combine the stock, buckwheat, carrots, celery, garlic and half of the parsley in the bowl of the slow cooker. Cover and cook for 3 hours, until the buckwheat is tender.

Heat the olive oil in a large frying pan over high heat. Add the leek and fry for a couple of minutes, until soft. Stir through the mushrooms, season to taste with salt and pepper and cook for 5 minutes, just until the mushrooms have collapsed. Tip the contents of the frying pan into the slow cooker and give it a quick stir. Cover and cook for 1 hour.

Scatter with the remaining parsley to serve.

Curried cauliflower, celeriac and yoghurt soup

SERVES 4
PREPARATION 20 minutes
COOKING 5 hours

1 small cauliflower
1 small head celeriac,
    peeled and chopped
4 cloves garlic, chopped
4 cups (1 litre) vegetable
    stock
2 tablespoons mild curry
    powder
1 tablespoon cornflour
1 cup (260 g) Greek-style
    yoghurt
handful chervil or small
    coriander (cilantro) leaves
toasted wholemeal naan
    bread, to serve

● VEGETARIAN

If turnip and celery were to have a child, it might look like celeriac – a rather unattractive child, it must be said. But what this gnarled-looking root vegetable lacks in looks, it more than makes up for in flavour. In winter it's everywhere, and pretty cheap too, so snap some up to make this amazing soup.

Heat your slow cooker to High.

Remove any leaves and woody parts of the stem from the cauliflower and discard. Roughly chop the cauliflower into large florets and put into the bowl of the slow cooker, along with the celeriac and garlic.

In a bowl, combine the stock, curry powder and cornflour, then pour into the slow cooker. Cover and cook for 4 hours, until the vegetables are tender.

Use a stick blender to blitz until smooth. Alternatively, transfer the soup in batches to a food processor and process until smooth, then return to the slow cooker.

Stir through the yoghurt. Cover and cook for 1 hour, until the soup is heated through and the flavours have developed.

Transfer to four large bowls. Scatter with the chervil or coriander and serve with toasted naan bread.

Barley, spinach and porcini soup

SERVES 4
PREPARATION 10 minutes
COOKING 3½ hours

1 cup (200 g) pearl barley
¼ cup (50 g) brown basmati
   rice
8 cups (2 litres) vegetable
   stock
1 small onion, finely chopped
1 clove garlic, finely chopped
1 carrot, finely chopped
2 stalks celery, trimmed and
   finely chopped
¾ cup (30 g) chopped dried
   porcini mushrooms
large handful flat-leaf
   parsley, finely chopped
4 large handfuls baby
   spinach leaves
1 cup (100 g) finely grated
   parmesan
rye bread, to serve

● VEGETARIAN

I do like throwing dried mushrooms into my slow cooker at any opportunity. They add tonnes of savoury flavour and meaty richness. Although they used to be a bit of a posh ingredient, they can be picked up at most supermarkets these days. This soup is finished off with a decent sprinkling of parmesan – another ingredient I use whenever I can!

Heat your slow cooker to High.

Put the barley, rice, stock, onion, garlic, carrot, celery, mushrooms and half of the parsley into the bowl of the slow cooker. Season generously with salt and pepper, then give everything a good stir. Cover and cook for 3 hours.

Stir through the spinach, the rest of the parsley and half of the parmesan. Cover and cook for 30 minutes, until the barley is tender and the spinach has wilted.

Ladle the soup into bowls and scatter with the remaining parmesan. Serve with rye bread on the side.

Lebanese chickpea and parsley soup

SERVES 4
PREPARATION 25 minutes
COOKING 2½ hours

400 g (14 oz) can chickpeas, rinsed and well drained
400 g (14 oz) can crushed tomatoes
4 cups (1 litre) vegetable stock
1 teaspoon dried thyme
2 teaspoons ground cumin
¼ cup (55 g) fine burghul
large handful finely chopped curly parsley
1 red onion, finely chopped
2 tablespoons olive oil
handful thinly sliced mint
2 little gem lettuces, leaves separated
lemon cheeks, to serve

● VEGAN

This is almost like tabbouleh in soup form, and very delicious and fresh it is too. The lettuce leaves can either be stirred through the hot soup to wilt them, or treated as a novel way to scoop up and eat the chickpeas.

Heat your slow cooker to High.

Put the chickpeas, tomatoes, stock, thyme and cumin into the bowl of the slow cooker. Season generously with salt and pepper, then give everything a good stir. Cover and cook for 2 hours, until the chickpeas are tender and the flavours have developed.

Stir through the burghul, parsley, onion and half of the olive oil. Cover and cook for 30 minutes, until the burghul is soft.

Stir through the mint, then serve the soup in bowls with lettuce leaves and lemon cheeks on the side.

As you eat, dunk the lettuce leaves in the soup, allowing them to wilt and soften, and adding a squeeze of lemon juice and a drizzle of the remaining olive oil to taste.

Persian lentil soup with rice and noodles

SERVES 6
PREPARATION 20 minutes
COOKING 3 hours

400 g (14 oz) can brown
    lentils
400 g (14 oz) can fava beans
400 g (14 oz) can cannellini
    beans
6 cups (1.5 litres) vegetable
    stock
400 g (14 oz) can cherry
    tomatoes
2 tablespoons tomato paste
    (concentrated purée)
1 teaspoon ground cumin
½ teaspoon ground cinnamon
½ teaspoon dried mint
large handful finely chopped
    flat-leaf parsley
⅓ cup (65 g) basmati rice
⅔ cup (60 g) egg vermicelli
    noodles, broken into
    2–3 cm (¾–1¼ in) lengths
extra virgin olive oil, to serve
lemon wedges, to serve

● VEGETARIAN

This softly spiced soup is full of goodness. A version of this soup is traditionally served on the eve of the Persian New Year. The noodles are said to bring good fortune, and the combination of legumes, beans and rice make this a hearty and nourishing meal.

Heat your slow cooker to High.

Put the lentils and beans into a colander and rinse under the cold tap, using your hands to separate them. Shake dry, then tip into the bowl of the slow cooker. Add the stock, tomatoes, tomato paste, cumin, cinnamon, mint and parsley. Season generously with salt and pepper, then give everything a good stir. Cover and cook for 2 hours.

Stir through the rice and noodles, then cover and cook for 1 hour, until both rice and noodles are cooked through.

Ladle the soup into bowls and drizzle with olive oil. Serve with lemon wedges on the side for squeezing into the soup.

Three sisters soup

SERVES 4
PREPARATION 10 minutes
COOKING 3 hours

2 corn cobs, husks removed
400 g (14 oz) can red kidney
    beans
400 g (14 oz) can cannellini
    beans
4 cups (1 litre) vegetable
    stock
400 g (14 oz) can crushed
    tomatoes
1 cup (150 g) cubed pumpkin
2 cloves garlic, crushed
2 teaspoons ground cumin
1 teaspoon dried oregano
½ teaspoon chilli powder
large handful green beans,
    cut into 2–3 cm (¾–1¼ in)
    lengths
1 tablespoon olive oil

● VEGAN
● GLUTEN-FREE

Native Americans think of beans, corn and squash (pumpkin) as being three sisters, because the crops grow close to each other, like sisters. The fresh corn adds an unmistakable texture and flavour to this robust soup.

Heat your slow cooker to High.

Cut the corn kernels from the cobs. Put the canned beans into a colander and rinse under the cold tap, using your hands to separate the beans. Shake them dry, then tip into the bowl of the slow cooker. Add the corn, stock, tomatoes, pumpkin, garlic, cumin, oregano, chilli powder and a generous seasoning of salt and pepper. Give everything a good stir to combine, then cover and cook for 2 hours.

Stir through the green beans, then quickly cover again to avoid losing too much heat. Cook for 1 hour, until all the vegetables are tender.

Serve in large bowls with a drizzle of olive oil.

Moroccan carrot and oat soup with ras el hanout

SERVES 4
PREPARATION 25 minutes
COOKING 4 hours

8 cups (2 litres) vegetable stock
4 carrots, peeled and finely chopped
1 potato, peeled and finely chopped
½ cup (50 g) traditional (not quick-cooking) rolled oats
1 small brown onion, finely chopped
2 cloves garlic, finely chopped
1 teaspoon ground ginger
2 teaspoons ras el hanout
3 tablespoons tomato paste (concentrated purée)
small bunch coriander (cilantro), leaves and stems roughly chopped
2 tablespoons honey
1 tablespoon toasted sesame seeds
yoghurt (optional), to serve

● VEGETARIAN

Whether bought in Moroccan spice markets or your local supermarket, ras el hanout means 'top shelf' – so called because it was originally a house blend of many exotic spices, unique to each spice merchant. Here it adds fragrant depth to sweet, slow-cooked carrots. If you want to make this vegan, just serve the soup as is, without the yoghurt.

Heat your slow cooker to High.

Put the stock, carrots, potato, oats, onion, garlic, ginger, ras el hanout and tomato paste in the bowl of the slow cooker. Season generously with salt and pepper, then give everything a good stir. Cover and cook for 4 hours, until the carrots are very tender.

Use a stick blender to blitz the soup until it is thick and smooth. Alternatively, transfer the soup in batches to a food processor and process until thick and smooth, then return to the slow cooker.

Stir through the coriander and ladle into large bowls. Drizzle with the honey and scatter with the sesame seeds. Serve with a dollop of yoghurt, if you like.

French leek soup with ricotta toasts

SERVES 4
PREPARATION 20 minutes
COOKING about 3 hours

2 tablespoons olive oil
2 large leeks, thinly sliced
4 cloves garlic, finely chopped
2 teaspoons thyme leaves
1 bay leaf
6 cups (1.5 litres) vegetable
   stock
2 tablespoons Worcestershire
   sauce
1 tablespoon cornflour
4 slices rye bread
½ cup (115 g) low-fat ricotta
1 tablespoon snipped chives
handful roughly chopped
   flat-leaf parsley

● VEGETARIAN

I guess this is a health-conscious version of French onion soup, without all the butter. The leeks are lightly sweated off in a pan before being slowly cooked, rendering them sweet and silky soft. Feel free to dunk the ricotta toast into your bowl of soup or, if your bowl is big enough, float it on the top.

Heat your slow cooker to High.

Heat the oil in a frying pan over high heat and fry the leeks, garlic and thyme for 4–5 minutes, until the leeks have just collapsed. Tip into the bowl of the slow cooker, then add the bay leaf, stock, Worcestershire sauce and cornflour. Give everything a good stir, making sure the cornflour has dissolved, then cover and cook for 3 hours, until the leeks are very tender. Turn the slow cooker down to Low and leave covered while you make the ricotta toasts.

Toast the bread until golden on both sides, then spread with the ricotta.

Ladle the soup into bowls and scatter with the chives and parsley. Serve with the ricotta toasts on the side.

Mixed pea and bean soup with za'atar

SERVES 4
PREPARATION 20 minutes
COOKING 4 hours

2 cups (500 g) dried pea and bean soup mix
8 cups (2 litres) vegetable stock
1 cup (250 ml) tomato passata (puréed tomatoes)
2 small carrots, peeled and thinly sliced
1 stalk celery, thinly sliced
3 cloves garlic, finely chopped
small handful finely chopped flat-leaf parsley
2 bay leaves
1 tablespoon olive oil
za'atar, to serve

● VEGAN
● GLUTEN-FREE

The inspiration for this was right under my nose on the shelf at my local supermarket. This recipe makes good use of a bag of pre-mixed dried peas and beans called 'soup mix'. I've grown up with this as the main ingredient in many home-cooked soups, stews and casseroles. The addition of za'atar brings an exotic touch to the soup. This ready-made Middle Eastern mixed spice and sesame seed blend is perfect for sprinkling on boiled eggs, flatbread doused in olive oil – and, of course, soups!

Heat your slow cooker to High.

Combine the dried peas and beans, stock, tomato passata, carrot, celery, garlic, parsley, bay leaves and olive oil in the bowl of the slow cooker. Season generously with salt and pepper, then give everything a good stir. Cover and cook for 4 hours, until the peas and beans are tender.

Ladle the soup into bowls and sprinkle with za'atar to taste.

Spicy Korean kimchi and tofu soup

SERVES 4
PREPARATION 15 minutes
COOKING about 3 hours

1 tablespoon vegetable oil
1 brown onion, sliced
1 cup (200 g) roughly chopped kimchi
2 cloves garlic, crushed
1 tablespoon finely grated ginger
¼ teaspoon chilli powder
8 small fresh shiitake mushrooms
375 g (13 oz) can sliced bamboo shoots, well drained
300 g (10½ oz) marinated firm tofu, thickly sliced
1 cup (250 ml) vegetable stock
1 tablespoon gluten-free tamari
1 tablespoon mirin
2 tomatoes, roughly chopped

● VEGAN
● GLUTEN-FREE

Kimchi not only ticks all the boxes in terms of on-point, fashionable food, but also boasts a list of health benefits as long as your arm. When an ingredient packs this much punch, you don't need to mess around with it too much. For a really quick meal, it's delicious simply stirred through some steamed rice. But with just a little more effort, and a slow cooker, you can make this amazing soupy stew, with plump tomatoes and shiitake mushrooms floating happily in a spicy broth.

Heat your slow cooker to High.

Heat the vegetable oil in a frying pan over high heat. Add the onion and fry for 3–4 minutes, until golden. Stir through the kimchi, garlic, ginger and chilli powder, then set aside.

Put the mushrooms, bamboo shoots and tofu into the bowl of the slow cooker. Scrape the onion mixture from the frying pan over the mushrooms, then pour in the stock, tamari and mirin. Cover and cook for 2 hours.

Stir in the tomatoes, then quickly cover again to avoid losing too much heat. Cook for 1 hour, until the tomatoes are soft and collapsed.

Ladle into bowls to serve.

Lentil, spinach and sun-dried tomato soup

SERVES 4
PREPARATION 20 minutes
COOKING 3 hours

2 cups (410 g) split red lentils
8 cups (2 litres) vegetable
    stock
½ cup (75 g) sun-dried
    tomatoes
100 g (3½ oz) baby kale
    leaves
3 spring onions (scallions),
    thinly sliced
½ teaspoon ground turmeric
1 teaspoon dried oregano
small handful finely chopped
    flat-leaf parsley
1 tablespoon olive oil

● VEGAN
● GLUTEN-FREE

Sun-dried tomatoes give sweetness and colour, but they won't break down during cooking like fresh tomatoes do. Despite the restrained use of spice here, the soup has a surprising amount of oomph. If you're not making this gluten-free, it would be lovely mopped up with hot naan bread or any Indian-style flatbread.

Heat your slow cooker to High.

Combine the lentils, stock, sun-dried tomatoes, kale, spring onions, turmeric, oregano and a generous seasoning of salt and pepper in the bowl of the slow cooker. Cover and cook for 3 hours, until the lentils and vegetables are tender.

Ladle the soup into large bowls, scatter with the parsley and drizzle with the olive oil.

Curry Night

Spinach and pea paneer

SERVES 4
PREPARATION 15 minutes
COOKING about 3 hours

750 g (1 lb 10 oz) frozen
   spinach
1 cup (140 g) frozen peas
1 tablespoon vegetable oil
1 brown onion, finely chopped
4 garlic cloves, roughly
   chopped
2 tablespoons roughly
   chopped ginger
2 teaspoons ground cumin
2 teaspoons ground coriander
½ teaspoon garam masala
½ teaspoon chilli powder
1 teaspoon fine sea salt
150 g (5½ oz) baby spinach
   leaves
2 teaspoons olive oil
400 g (14 oz) paneer, cubed
brown basmati rice, to serve

● VEGETARIAN
● GLUTEN-FREE

This gentle curry makes you feel better with every mouthful. Like frozen peas, frozen spinach is a truly healthy convenience food, and it seems to have been just made for the slow cooker. It can come in little frozen blocks or loosely packed. Either variety is fine. This recipe is bursting with green goodness, and comes in three easy parts: slow cook the spinach, add the curry spices, then whiz it all up and serve it with pan-fried golden paneer. For texture, I like to leave the peas a tad chunky.

Heat your slow cooker to High.

Combine the frozen spinach and half of the peas in the bowl of the slow cooker. Cover and cook for 2 hours, giving it a stir halfway through.

Heat the vegetable oil in a small saucepan over medium–high heat. Add the onion, garlic and ginger to the pan and cook for 8–10 minutes, until golden. Stir in the spices, then scrape into the slow cooker. Add the salt, fresh spinach and remaining peas, then cover and cook for 30 minutes, until the fresh spinach has wilted and is tender.

Use a stick blender to blitz the curry – I like to keep it slightly chunky in texture. Alternatively, transfer in batches to a food processor and process until chunky and thick, then return to the slow cooker. Turn the slow cooker down to Low and leave covered while you fry the paneer.

Heat the olive oil in a non-stick frying pan over high heat. Add the paneer and cook for 1 minute each side until golden.

Serve the spinach and pea curry on a bed of rice, with the golden paneer on the side.

Yellow curry of pumpkin, prawns and pineapple

SERVES 4
PREPARATION 20 minutes
COOKING 3½ hours

¼ cup (55 g) Thai yellow curry
   paste
1 cup (250 ml) light coconut
   milk
1 cup (250 ml) vegetable
   stock
1 tablespoon cornflour
1 tablespoon fish sauce
1 tablespoon brown sugar
6 kaffir lime leaves
2 stalks lemongrass,
   white parts only
1 small sweet potato, cut into
   1 cm (½ in) thick rounds
400 g (14 oz) jap pumpkin,
   skin on, cut into wedges
200 g (7 oz) fresh pineapple,
   cut into small wedges
8 cherry tomatoes
36 raw prawns, about 500 g
   (1 lb 2 oz) in total, peeled
   and deveined, but with
   tails intact
handful mixed Asian herbs,
   such as coriander
   (cilantro), mint and
   Thai basil
¼ cup (35 g) roasted peanuts

● GLUTEN-FREE

There is a wide range of Thai curry pastes out there. The best way to choose a good one is simply to look for those made in Thailand. The Thai brands are generally more finely processed into a paste, so you need less and they keep for ages in the fridge. This also makes them a wise economical choice, but be warned – they are often very spicy!

Heat your slow cooker to High.

Combine the curry paste, coconut milk, stock, cornflour, fish sauce, brown sugar and lime leaves in the bowl of the slow cooker. Smash the lemongrass stalks with a rolling pin and add to the bowl. Give everything a good stir, making sure the cornflour has dissolved. Don't worry if the curry paste doesn't completely dissolve – it will do so as it cooks.

Add the sweet potato, pumpkin, pineapple and tomatoes to the slow cooker. Cover and cook for 2 hours, until the sauce is gently bubbling around the edges.

Working quickly to avoid losing too much heat, stir gently, being careful not to break up the vegetables. Cover and cook for 1 hour, until the vegetables are very tender.

Tumble the prawns into the slow cooker, gently nudging them into the curry. Quickly cover again and cook for 30 minutes, until the prawns are pink and cooked through.

Transfer the curry to four bowls and scatter with the herbs and peanuts.

Sri Lankan cashew curry

SERVES 4
PREPARATION 15 minutes
COOKING about 3 hours

2 cups (310 g) roasted
   cashews
400 g (14 oz) can crushed
   tomatoes
2 tablespoons tomato paste
   (concentrated purée)
1 tablespoon olive oil
1 brown onion, chopped
2 cloves garlic, chopped
1 tablespoon finely grated
   ginger
1 stem curry leaves
   (about 24)
1 stick cinnamon
1 teaspoon ground cumin
½ teaspoon ground turmeric
¼ teaspoon chilli powder
1 cup (250 ml) light coconut
   milk
handful roughly chopped
   coriander (cilantro)
Sri Lankan red rice or brown
   basmati rice and lime
   wedges, to serve

● VEGAN
● GLUTEN-FREE

As if cashews aren't moreish enough already, they are taken to another level in this simple, tasty curry. Roasting nuts, and whole spices for that matter, helps to draw out their oils and add flavour. You could roast your own cashews in a moderate oven until they are golden. But seriously, how good are shop-bought salted and roasted cashews? I buy them by the kilo: it's more economical, and they're always good to have on hand. Because I'm lucky enough to live near a store specialising in Sri Lankan foods – and the owner is very good at selling me all sorts of exotic treats – I often serve this curry with red rice, but brown basmati has a similarly nutty taste and chewy texture.

Heat your slow cooker to High.

Combine the cashews, tomatoes and tomato paste in the bowl of the slow cooker.

Heat the olive oil in a frying pan over high heat and cook the onion, garlic and ginger for 2–3 minutes, until softened. Stir in the curry leaves, letting them sizzle and cook for a minute. Scrape the contents of the frying pan into the slow cooker, then add the cinnamon, cumin, turmeric, chilli powder and coconut milk. Season generously with salt and pepper, then give everything a good stir. Cover and cook for 2 hours.

Give it a stir, then quickly cover again to avoid losing too much heat. Cook for 1 hour, until the curry is aromatic and the cashews are slightly tender. Stir through half of the coriander.

Serve the curry on a bed of rice, scattered with the remaining coriander, and with lime wedges for squeezing.

Vietnamese chicken and sweet potato curry

SERVES 4
PREPARATION 30 minutes
COOKING 3 hours

500 g (1 lb 2 oz) sweet
 potatoes, peeled and
 cut into cubes
2 carrots, peeled and cut
 into thick slices
1 small bunch coriander
 (cilantro)
2 stalks lemongrass, white
 parts only, roughly chopped
3 cloves garlic, finely chopped
1 tablespoon finely grated
 ginger
1 tablespoon fish sauce
2 tablespoons mild curry
 powder
2 teaspoons cornflour
2 cups (500 ml) chicken
 stock
8 skinless chicken drumsticks
3 star anise

● GLUTEN-FREE

If you're a novice when it comes to cooking Asian food, then Vietnamese cuisine, with its clean, fresh flavours, is a good place to start. And this comforting meal in a bowl couldn't be easier. Chicken drumsticks will give you the extra chickeny flavour that comes from being cooked on the bone, and can sometimes be found without their skin. If you have no luck, it's easily removed: use a large knife or Chinese cleaver to make a 1cm (½ in) nick in the skin at one end, then pull off and discard. If that sounds too faffy, you could always use chicken breast, tenderloin or lean thigh fillets instead – all three will do a nice job here.

Heat your slow cooker to High.

Tumble the sweet potatoes and carrots in the bowl of the slow cooker.

Take the bunch of coriander, scrape the roots clean and wash well to remove any dirt. Roughly chop the roots and some of the stems, then set aside the remainder of the bunch.

In a food processor, combine the chopped coriander roots and stems with the lemongrass, garlic, ginger, fish sauce, curry powder, cornflour and stock and process to a paste. Scrape into a bowl and add the chicken and star anise. Toss to coat the chicken thoroughly.

Arrange the chicken over the vegetables in the slow cooker, then pour in the sauce from the bowl. Cover and cook for 2 hours. Working quickly to avoid losing too much heat, turn each piece of chicken over, then cover and cook for 1 hour, until it is cooked through.

Meanwhile, roughly chop the reserved coriander stems and leaves. Transfer the curry to a serving dish, then ladle into big bowls and scatter with the chopped coriander.

Simple yellow dahl

SERVES 4
PREPARATION 20 minutes
COOKING about 3½ hours

1 tablespoon olive oil
1 brown onion, chopped
2 large green chillies, cut
    in half lengthways
3 cm (1¼ in) piece ginger,
    coarsely grated
4 cloves garlic, roughly
    chopped
1 stem curry leaves
    (about 24)
1 teaspoon cumin seeds
½ teaspoon black mustard
    seeds
½ teaspoon chilli powder
½ teaspoon ground turmeric
1¼ cups (255 g) yellow lentils
    (or split peas)
400 ml (14 fl oz) can light
    coconut milk
8 cups (2 litres) vegetable
    stock
3 large handfuls baby spinach
    leaves
large handful coriander
    (cilantro), roughly chopped,
    plus extra leaves, to serve
crispy fried shallots, to serve

● VEGAN
● GLUTEN-FREE

Dahl does double duty as a soup or a hearty meal, and of course either is a healthy option. This may seem like a crazy amount of liquid at first, but lentils are like a sponge and will soak it all up. Mental note: any leftovers are excellent reheated and served with rice or flatbread.

Heat your slow cooker to High.

Heat the olive oil in a frying pan over high heat. Add the onions and fry for about 5 minutes, until soft. Add the green chillies, ginger, garlic and curry leaves and cook for just a minute to soften them without burning. Stir in the cumin seeds, mustard seeds, chilli powder and turmeric until well combined, then remove from the heat.

Scrape the contents of the frying pan into the bowl of the slow cooker. Add the lentils, coconut milk and stock and season generously with salt and pepper. Give everything a good stir, then cover and cook for 3 hours.

Stir through the spinach and chopped coriander, then quickly cover again to avoid losing too much heat. Cook for a further 30 minutes, until the spinach has wilted.

Serve in bowls, garnished with the extra coriander leaves, and with crispy fried shallots on the side.

Root vegetable korma

SERVES 4
PREPARATION 30 minutes
COOKING 4 hours

300 g (10½ oz) pumpkin
1 bunch Dutch (baby) carrots
4 small waxy potatoes, such
    as kipfler, halved lengthways
1 parsnip, peeled and cut
    into 8 pieces
1 cup (260 g) natural yoghurt
4 green cardamom pods
4 cloves
1 stick cinnamon, broken up
1 cup (250 ml) vegetable stock
1 tablespoon cornflour
handful coriander (cilantro)
    leaves
¼ cup (25 g) toasted flaked
    almonds
basmati rice, to serve

KORMA PASTE
½ cup (50 g) toasted flaked
    almonds
1 brown onion, roughly chopped
1 clove garlic, roughly chopped
2 teaspoons finely grated ginger
2 teaspoons ground cumin
2 teaspoons ground coriander
1 teaspoon garam masala
½ teaspoon ground turmeric
½ teaspoon chilli powder
1 tablespoon olive oil
1 tablespoon tomato paste
    (concentrated purée)

● VEGETARIAN
● GLUTEN-FREE

A korma is a gently spiced curry that's usually enriched with cream, but this lighter version uses yoghurt and is fragrant with warm spices, including cardamom, cloves and cinnamon, as well as the usual, edgier suspects like cumin and chilli powder. Root vegetables take much longer to cook than you might think in a slow cooker, making it even more important not to be tempted to lift the lid and have a peek. I like to leave the skin on the pumpkin for colour and texture, but you can peel it, if you prefer. Feel free to use a bought korma paste as a shortcut.

To make the korma paste, simply put all the paste ingredients into a food processor and process for a few seconds. Scrape down the bowl and process again. Do this a couple more times until you have a thick, smooth paste. Set aside. If you are super-organised, you could make this a few hours or even a day in advance and keep it in a covered bowl in the fridge.

Heat your slow cooker to High.

Scoop out and discard the seeds from the pumpkin, then cut into chunky wedges. Trim the carrots. Place the pumpkin, carrots, potatoes and parsnip in the bowl of the slow cooker.

In a bowl, combine the korma paste, yoghurt, cardamom, cloves, cinnamon, vegetable stock and cornflour and mix well. Scrape into the slow cooker, on top of the vegetables.

Cover and cook for 2 hours. Give everything a stir, then quickly cover again to avoid losing too much heat. Turn the slow cooker down to Low and cook for a further 2 hours, until all the vegetables are tender.

Transfer to a serving dish and scatter with the coriander leaves and flaked almonds. Serve with rice.

Black and white chana masala

SERVES 4
PREPARATION 20 minutes
SOAKING overnight
COOKING about 4 hours

---

1 cup (250 g) dried black
　　chickpeas
400 g (14 oz) can chickpeas,
　　rinsed and well drained
2 cups (500 ml) tomato
　　passata (puréed tomatoes)
1 tablespoon olive oil
1 red onion, sliced into
　　wedges
2 tablespoons coarsely
　　grated ginger
3 cloves garlic, finely chopped
2 large red chillies, split
　　lengthways
1 stem curry leaves
　　(about 24)
2 teaspoons cumin seeds
1 teaspoon brown mustard
　　seeds
2 teaspoons ground coriander
1 teaspoon garam masala
1 teaspoon fine sea salt
12 small papadams, to serve

● VEGAN
● GLUTEN-FREE

Chana masala is a simple chickpea curry and recipes for it abound, but here the inclusion of black chickpeas switches it up a bit. These are smaller and firmer than 'white' chickpeas, with a mild smoky flavour. They need an overnight soak before cooking, though, so if you are feeling less inspired or lacking time, simply use another can of regular chickpeas.

Soak the black chickpeas in a bowl of cold water overnight. Next day, drain and put into a saucepan. Cover with cold water and boil for 1 hour, topping up with water as needed, until the chickpeas are just tender.

Heat your slow cooker to High.

Drain the black chickpeas well and tip into the bowl of the slow cooker, along with the canned chickpeas, tomato passata and 1 cup (250 ml) water. Give everything a good stir, then cover and cook for 2 hours.

Towards the end of the 2 hours, heat the olive oil in a frying pan over high heat. Add the onion, ginger, garlic, chillies, curry leaves, cumin seeds, mustard seeds, coriander and garam masala and cook, stirring, for about 1 minute, until fragrant. Pour in ¼ cup (60 ml) water, stir to incorporate any stuck-on bits and then scrape the contents of the frying pan into the slow cooker. Add the salt and give everything a good stir, then cover and cook for 1 hour, until the sauce has thickened.

Serve the chana masala with papadams.

Black-eyed bean curry

SERVES 4
PREPARATION 20 minutes
SOAKING overnight
COOKING about 4 hours

1 cup (185 g) dried
    black-eyed beans
1 brown onion, finely chopped
400 g (14 oz) can cherry
    tomatoes
3 cloves garlic, finely chopped
1 tablespoon finely grated
    ginger
¼ teaspoon ground turmeric
1 teaspoon mild chilli powder
2 teaspoons ground coriander
1 teaspoon garam masala
1 tablespoon olive oil
1 teaspoon cumin seeds
½ teaspoon black mustard
    seeds
6 green cardamom pods,
    lightly crushed
4–6 dried chillies
large handful chopped
    coriander (cilantro)

● VEGAN
● GLUTEN-FREE

A much-loved ingredient in soul food, these little dried beans (also called black-eyed peas) can be identified by their little black spot, which resembles an eye. In Southern cooking, they are often sautéed with collard greens and smoked ham – and very delicious this is too – but their bold earthiness also stands up well to heavily spiced Indian flavours.

Soak the beans in a bowl of cold water overnight. Drain well and set aside.

Heat your slow cooker to High.

Put the black-eyed beans, onion, tomatoes, garlic, ginger, turmeric, chilli powder, ground coriander, garam masala and 3 cups (750 ml) water into the bowl of the slow cooker. Give everything a good stir and season generously with salt and pepper. Cover and cook for 4 hours, until the beans are tender and the sauce is gently simmering around the edges.

Transfer to a large serving dish. Put the olive oil into a small frying pan over high heat and add the cumin seeds, mustard seeds, cardamom pods and dried chillies. When the seeds start to sizzle, pour the oil and spices over the curry, then scatter with the chopped coriander.

Lamb and one hundred almond curry

SERVES 4
PREPARATION 20 minutes
COOKING about 4 hours

750 g (1 lb 10 oz) lamb leg
    steaks
1 tablespoon olive oil
1 red onion, roughly chopped
4 cloves garlic, roughly
    chopped
5 cm (2 in) piece ginger,
    finely chopped
2 large green chillies,
    thinly sliced
1½ cups (190 g) slivered
    almonds
2 teaspoons ground cumin
2 teaspoons ground coriander
1 teaspoon garam masala
½ teaspoon ground cinnamon
5 green cardamom pods,
    lightly crushed
1 cup (260 g) natural yoghurt
2 teaspoons beef stock
    powder
2 teaspoons cornflour
handful chopped coriander
    (cilantro), to serve
basmati rice, to serve

● GLUTEN-FREE

One hundred here simply means a lot! And when it comes to almonds, it makes sense to be generous so you get the crunch and flavour of the nuts with every mouthful of this luscious lamb curry. Look for almonds sold in bulk at health-food stores.

Heat your slow cooker to High.

Trim all the fat from the lamb and discard. Cut the meat into 4–5 cm (1½–2 in) chunks and put into the bowl of the slow cooker.

Put the olive oil into a frying pan over high heat. When the oil is hot, add the onion, garlic, ginger, chillies and almonds and fry for 2–3 minutes, until the almonds are golden. Add the cumin, ground coriander, garam masala, cinnamon and cardamom and cook for a minute, stirring, until fragrant. Remove from the heat and stir in the yoghurt.

In a bowl or jug, combine the stock powder and cornflour with ½ cup (125 ml) water. Stir into the almond mixture, then pour the whole lot over the lamb in the slow cooker. Cover and cook for 3 hours.

Working quickly to avoid losing too much heat, turn the lamb over, then cover and cook for 1 hour, until the meat is very tender.

Use a slotted spoon to transfer the lamb to a serving dish and pour some of the sauce over the top. Scatter the curry with chopped coriander and serve with basmati rice.

Lamb, eggplant and chickpea curry

SERVES 4
PREPARATION 20 minutes
COOKING about 3½ hours

1 tablespoon olive oil
1 large brown onion,
    thinly sliced
1 teaspoon fine sea salt
2 teaspoons ground cumin
2 teaspoons ground coriander
½ teaspoon ground turmeric
1 teaspoon dried mint
750 g (1 lb 10 oz) diced
    lean lamb
½ cup (130 g) natural
    yoghurt
¼ cup (30 g) chickpea flour
    (besan)
400 g (14 oz) can chickpeas,
    rinsed and well drained
1 eggplant (aubergine),
    cut into chunks
brown basmati rice, to serve
lemon wedges, to serve

● GLUTEN-FREE

Chickpea flour, or besan, is used to make various batters in Indian and Middle Eastern cooking. Here, it is mixed with yoghurt to add body to a hearty lamb and eggplant curry.

Heat your slow cooker to High.

Put the olive oil into a frying pan over high heat. When the oil is hot, add the onion and cook for 5 minutes, until golden. Sprinkle in the salt, cumin, coriander, turmeric and mint. Stir for a minute, then scrape the contents of the frying pan into the bowl of the slow cooker. Add the lamb and give everything a good stir, then cover and cook for 1½ hours.

In a bowl, mix together the yoghurt and chickpea flour until smooth. Add to the slow cooker, along with the chickpeas, and give everything a good stir. Tumble the eggplant on top, then cover and cook for 1 hour.

Give it a gentle stir, then quickly cover again to avoid losing too much heat. Cook for 1 hour, until the lamb is very tender.

Transfer to four bowls and serve with rice and lemon wedges.

Light butter chicken

SERVES 4
PREPARATION 20 minutes
COOKING about 4¼ hours

750 g (1 lb 10 oz) chicken
    thigh fillets
1 brown onion, chopped
3 cm (1¼ in) piece ginger,
    chopped
2 cloves garlic, chopped
1 large green chilli, seeded
    and chopped
1 tablespoon olive oil
1 tablespoon butter
½ teaspoon chilli powder
1 tablespoon ground cumin
1 tablespoon ground
    coriander
1 tablespoon garam masala
1 tablespoon sweet paprika
5 green cardamom pods,
    lightly crushed
2 tablespoons tomato paste
    (concentrated purée)
2 teaspoons chicken stock
    powder
400 g (14 oz) can crushed
    tomatoes
1 tablespoon cornflour
1 cup (260 g) natural yoghurt
brown basmati rice, to serve
handful roughly chopped
    coriander (cilantro)
lemon wedges, to serve

● GLUTEN-FREE

We all love butter chicken, but it can be a guilty pleasure. This version, however, is delicious and contains only a tablespoon of butter, which works out to be barely a teaspoon per person. So put aside any guilt and enjoy!

Heat your slow cooker to High.

Trim off all the fat from the chicken thighs and discard. Cut each thigh in half, or into thirds if large, bearing in mind that they will shrink as they cook. Refrigerate until needed.

Put the onion, ginger, garlic and chilli into a food processor and process until you have a chunky paste.

Heat the oil in a large frying pan over medium heat. Add the paste and cook for 8–10 minutes, until the liquid from the onion has evaporated and the paste looks dry. Stir through the butter and cook for a minute until the butter has melted. Stir in the chilli powder, cumin, coriander, garam masala, paprika and cardamom pods. Add 2 tablespoons cold water and stir to incorporate any stuck-on bits. Stir in the tomato paste and stock powder, then scrape the contents of the frying pan into the bowl of the slow cooker. Add the crushed tomatoes, cornflour, yoghurt and chicken. Give everything a good stir, nudging the chicken into the sauce, then cover and cook for 2 hours.

Give it a stir, then quickly cover again to avoid losing too much heat. Cook for a further 2 hours, until the chicken is very tender and the sauce is thick.

Serve the butter chicken on brown basmati rice, garnished with chopped coriander and with lemon wedges on the side.

Vegetable biryani with cranberries and pistachios

SERVES 4
PREPARATION 20 minutes
COOKING about 4 hours

4 small potatoes, scrubbed
200 g (7 oz) jap pumpkin, skin on
2 small carrots, scrubbed
½ cup (130 g) natural yoghurt
½ teaspoon saffron strands
1 tablespoon olive oil
1 red onion, thinly sliced
3 cloves garlic, finely chopped
1 tablespoon finely grated ginger
1 teaspoon cumin seeds
⅓ cup (50 g) roasted cashews
¼ cup (30 g) dried cranberries, plus 2 tablespoons extra
1 stick cinnamon
5 green cardamom pods, lightly crushed
1 teaspoon garam masala
1 cup (200 g) basmati rice, rinsed and drained
3 cups (750 ml) vegetable stock
¼ cup (30 g) roughly chopped pistachios
handful coriander (cilantro) leaves

● VEGETARIAN
● GLUTEN-FREE

There must be as many different versions of biryani as there are ways to spell it! Essentially a dish of slow-cooked basmati rice, it is heavily spiced, sweet and fragrant, often perfumed with a few drops of rosewater or orange flower water. Jewel-like cranberries are added for sweetness, and pistachios for their emerald colour and moreish, savoury crunch.

Cut the potatoes in half, then cut the pumpkin and carrots into chunks of about the same size. Put them all into a large bowl with the yoghurt and saffron. Mix well, then set aside for 30 minutes, stirring every now and then.

Meanwhile, heat your slow cooker to High.

Transfer the vegetables and yoghurt to the bowl of the slow cooker.

Heat the olive oil in a large frying pan over high heat. Add the onion and fry for 4–5 minutes, until starting to soften and turn golden. Add the garlic, ginger and cumin seeds and cook for a minute or so. Stir in the cashews, cranberries, cinnamon, cardamom and garam masala and cook for a minute, until fragrant. Add the rice and stir until it is glossy and well combined with the spice mixture. Pour in the stock, stirring to incorporate any stuck-on bits, then tip the whole lot into the slow cooker. Cover and cook for 3 hours.

Give everything a stir, then quickly cover again to avoid losing too much heat. Cook for 1 hour, until the rice is cooked through and the vegetables are tender.

Divide the biryani between four bowls. Scatter the pistachios and extra cranberries over the top, then garnish with the coriander leaves.

Chicken methi

SERVES 4
PREPARATION 20 minutes
COOKING about 3 hours

1 large brown onion, roughly
    chopped
3 cm (1¼ in) piece ginger,
    peeled and roughly
    chopped
4 cloves garlic, roughly
    chopped
1 teaspoon cumin seeds
1 red chilli, roughly chopped
1 tablespoon olive oil
small handful dried methi
    (fenugreek) leaves
2 teaspoons ground coriander
½ teaspoon ground turmeric
½ teaspoon chilli powder
½ teaspoon garam masala
1 teaspoon fine sea salt
1 cup (260 g) natural yoghurt
8 chicken tenderloins
1 large red chilli, seeded and
    thinly sliced
handful micro-coriander
    or regular coriander
    (cilantro) leaves
basmati rice, to serve

● GLUTEN-FREE

This exotic-sounding recipe takes its name from its dominant flavour, methi or fenugreek leaves - which are available dried from most Indian speciality food stores. When you buy a bag, open it and you should smell zesty, almost sharp aromas. This pungency softens with cooking to make a surprisingly light, tangy curry.

Heat your slow cooker to High.

Combine the onion, ginger, garlic, cumin seeds and chopped chilli in a food processor and process to a paste, scraping down the bowl a couple of times.

Put the olive oil into a frying pan over medium–high heat. When the oil is hot, add the paste and cook for 8–10 minutes, stirring often, until golden and aromatic. Stir through the methi leaves, ground coriander, turmeric, chilli powder, garam masala and salt and cook for 1 minute.

Stir in the yoghurt, then scrape the whole lot into the bowl of the slow cooker. Add the chicken, nudging it into the sauce. Cover and cook for 2 hours.

Give everything a gentle stir, then quickly cover again to avoid losing too much heat. Cook for 1 hour, until the chicken is cooked through and the sauce is a rich golden colour.

Transfer to a serving dish and garnish with the chilli and coriander leaves. Serve with basmati rice.

Ladakhi chicken

SERVES 4
PREPARATION 20 minutes
COOKING about 4 hours

6 chicken thigh fillets
1 large brown onion, roughly
   chopped
4 cloves garlic, roughly
   chopped
1 tablespoon finely grated
   ginger
2 large green chillies, roughly
   chopped
1 teaspoon fine sea salt
¼ teaspoon ground black
   pepper
2 tablespoons olive oil
400 g (14 oz) can crushed
   tomatoes
1 teaspoon ground cumin
½ teaspoon chilli powder
½ teaspoon mustard seeds
½ teaspoon cumin seeds
wild rice (or basmati rice),
   to serve
handful coriander (cilantro)
   leaves

● GLUTEN-FREE

High in the Himalayas, the Ladakh region of India is known for its stark, mountainous landscapes and colourful festivals. The food is influenced by neighbouring Tibet and Kashmir, with simple ingredients and pungent, peppery flavours.

Trim off all the fat from the chicken and discard. Cut each thigh in half, then refrigerate until needed.

Heat your slow cooker to High.

Put the onion, garlic, ginger, chillies, salt and pepper into a food processor. Pour in 1 tablespoon of the olive oil and process, scraping down the bowl a couple of times, until you have a smooth paste. Scrape into the bowl of the slow cooker. Add the tomatoes, cumin and chilli powder, then cover and cook for 2 hours, to allow the flavours to develop.

Working quickly to avoid losing too much heat, give the sauce a good stir, then add the chicken, gently nudging it into the sauce to coat well. Cover and cook for a further 2 hours, until the chicken is white and cooked through and the sauce is thick. Turn the slow cooker down to Low and leave covered.

Put the remaining olive oil into a small frying pan over high heat and add the mustard seeds and cumin seeds. When the seeds start to pop and sizzle, pour the oil and seeds over the chicken in the slow cooker and stir through.

Serve the Ladakhi chicken on a bed of wild rice, garnished with coriander leaves.

Cauliflower and chickpea curry with fennel seeds

SERVES 4
PREPARATION 20 minutes
COOKING about 3 hours

1 small head cauliflower,
  broken into florets
400 g (14 oz) can chickpeas,
  rinsed and well drained
1 tablespoon olive oil
1 red onion, chopped
2 cloves garlic, finely chopped
1 tablespoon finely grated
  ginger
2 large green chillies, sliced
  at an angle
2 teaspoons fennel seeds
1 teaspoon brown mustard
  seeds
1 stem curry leaves
  (about 24)
½ teaspoon chilli flakes
400 g (14 oz) can crushed
  tomatoes
1 teaspoon vegetable stock
  powder
lemon halves, to serve

● VEGAN
● GLUTEN-FREE

When people ask me about the best ingredients for slow cooking, I have to say that it is a close contest between canned tomatoes and canned chickpeas. With these in the cupboard, you'll always be able to throw together a simple, satisfying meal like this one, which uses both of these trusty standbys.

Heat your slow cooker to High.

Tumble the cauliflower and chickpeas into the bowl of the slow cooker.

Heat the olive oil in a frying pan over high heat. Add the onion, garlic, ginger and chilli and fry for a couple of minutes, until the onion has softened. Stir through the fennel seeds, mustard seeds and curry leaves. Cook until the seeds and leaves start to pop and sizzle, then tip into the slow cooker.

In a bowl, combine the chilli flakes, tomatoes, stock powder, ¼ cup (60 ml) water and a generous seasoning of salt and pepper, then pour into the slow cooker. Cover and cook for 3 hours, until the cauliflower is tender.

Serve with lemon halves on the side.

Green curry of tofu, bamboo shoots and eggplant

SERVES 4
PREPARATION 15 minutes
COOKING 4 hours

100 g (3½ oz) green beans,
  trimmed
2 green tomatoes, cut into
  wedges
125 g (4½ oz) baby corn
225 g (8 oz) can sliced
  bamboo shoots, drained
2 small Thai eggplants
  (aubergines), cut into
  wedges
300 g (10½ oz) firm tofu,
  cut into 2–3 cm (¾–1¼ in)
  pieces
2 tablespoons Thai green
  curry paste
1 cup (250 ml) light coconut
  milk
1 tablespoon fish sauce
1 tablespoon brown sugar
1 tablespoon cornflour
handful Thai basil leaves

● GLUTEN-FREE

A classic Thai green curry is full of fresh ingredients like lemongrass, red shallots, kaffir lime, coriander and, of course, green chilli. And a good curry paste will have all this ready to go in a couple of tablespoons, so that all you need do is add coconut milk and fresh vegetables. Green tomatoes make a pleasantly tart addition, cutting back the richness of the coconut milk.

Heat your slow cooker to High.

Put the green beans, green tomatoes, baby corn, bamboo shoots, eggplants and tofu into the bowl of the slow cooker.

In a bowl, combine the curry paste, coconut milk, fish sauce, brown sugar and cornflour, stirring to dissolve the sugar and cornflour. Pour into the slow cooker, then cover and cook for 2 hours.

Working quickly to avoid losing too much heat, give the curry a good stir. Cover and cook for a further 2 hours until all the vegetables are tender.

Transfer to a serving bowl and scatter with the basil leaves.

Lamb, chickpea and spinach curry

SERVES 6
PREPARATION 20 minutes
COOKING about 4½ hours

1 kg (2 lb 4 oz) lean lamb
1 brown onion, roughly
  chopped
3 cm (1¼ in) piece ginger,
  roughly chopped
2 cloves garlic, roughly
  chopped
1 large green chilli, seeded
  and roughly chopped
1 tablespoon olive oil
1 tablespoon ground
  coriander
1 tablespoon ground cumin
1 tablespoon garam masala
1 tablespoon sweet paprika
½ teaspoon chilli powder
5 green cardamom pods,
  lightly crushed
4 cloves
2 teaspoons chicken stock
  powder
1 cup (260 g) natural yoghurt
400 g (14 oz) can crushed
  tomatoes
1 tablespoon cornflour
400 g (14 oz) can chickpeas,
  rinsed and well drained
6 cups (270 g) baby spinach
  leaves
rice, to serve

● GLUTEN-FREE

Everything here – lean lamb, earthy chickpeas, tender spinach and heady spices – makes for a simply delicious curry.

Trim off all the fat from the lamb and discard. Cut the lamb into large bite-sized pieces and refrigerate until needed.

Heat your slow cooker to High.

Put the onion, ginger, garlic and chilli into a food processor and process to a chunky paste.

Heat the oil in a frying pan over medium heat. Add the paste and cook for 8–10 minutes, until the liquid from the onion has evaporated and the paste looks dry. Stir in the coriander, cumin, garam masala, paprika, chilli powder, cardamom and cloves. Add the stock powder and ½ cup (125 ml) water. Stir to incorporate any stuck-on bits, then remove from the heat.

Combine the yoghurt, tomatoes and cornflour in the bowl of the slow cooker, making sure the cornflour has dissolved. Tip in the contents of the frying pan, together with the lamb and chickpeas. Season generously with salt and pepper, then give everything a good stir. Cover and cook for 3 hours.

Working quickly to avoid losing too much heat, give it a quick stir, then cover and cook for 1 hour, until the lamb is tender.

Stir through the spinach, cover and cook for a further 30 minutes, until the spinach has wilted. Serve with your favourite rice.

Chicken, cashew and carrot curry

SERVES 4
PREPARATION 20 minutes
COOKING 5 hours

6 chicken thigh fillets
2 carrots, thickly sliced
165 ml (5¼ fl oz) can light
    coconut milk
2 brown onions, thinly sliced
2 cloves garlic, finely chopped
1 tablespoon finely chopped
    ginger
1 large red chilli, finely
    chopped
1 tablespoon ground
    coriander
2 teaspoons fennel seeds
½ teaspoon ground turmeric
1 teaspoon fine sea salt
½ cup (80 g) roasted
    cashews, plus a small
    handful extra
handful roughly chopped
    coriander (cilantro)

● **GLUTEN-FREE**

Chicken and cashews make such a lovely couple. And here the combination makes for a perfect no-fuss, high-impact curry, as everything is done in the slow cooker, with no paste-making or frying required.

Trim off all the fat from the chicken and discard. Cut each thigh in half, then refrigerate until needed.

Heat your slow cooker to High.

Combine the carrots, coconut milk, onions, garlic, ginger, chilli, ground coriander, fennel seeds, turmeric and salt in the bowl of the slow cooker. Cover and cook for 3 hours, stirring every hour.

Working quickly to avoid losing too much heat, add the chicken and cashews. Cover and cook for 2 hours, until the chicken is cooked through and the carrots are tender.

Stir in the chopped coriander and scatter with the extra cashews.

Saturday Night Specials

Prawns with fennel, saffron and ginger

SERVES 4
PREPARATION 20 minutes
COOKING about 2½ hours

---

1 large fennel bulb, preferably
    with feathery fronds intact
1 tablespoon olive oil
400 g (14 oz) can whole
    tomatoes
1 large red onion, thinly sliced
3 cm (1¼ in) piece ginger,
    coarsely grated
2 teaspoons smoked paprika
¼ teaspoon chilli powder
large pinch saffron strands
12 large raw prawns, shell on
handful coriander (cilantro)
    leaves
handful flat-leaf parsley
    leaves
steamed brown rice, to serve

● GLUTEN-FREE

This delicious, exotically spiced and luxurious recipe is actually quite simple to make. A slow cooker is surprisingly good at steaming seafood: fish fillets and prawns, layered on top of a bubbling hot sauce, cook surprisingly quickly. Prawns in the shell are used here, as the shells add extra flavour to the sauce as they cook and look more dramatic in the finished dish. Of course, peeled prawns can also be used – they will cook in about 15 minutes and are ready when they are pink and curled up.

Heat your slow cooker to High.

If the tops are still on the fennel, roughly chop some of the fronds and set aside. Thinly slice the fennel bulb lengthways from the base and put into a bowl. Add the olive oil, tomatoes, onion, ginger, paprika, chilli powder, saffron and a generous seasoning of salt and pepper. Give it a good stir, then tip into the slow cooker. Cover and cook for 2 hours, until the flavours have developed and the fennel is tender.

Working quickly to avoid losing too much heat, arrange the prawns on top of the fennel and tomato mixture. Cover and cook for 20 minutes, until the prawns are pink and cooked.

Serve on a bed of brown rice and garnish with the herbs.

Ratatouille with fish fillets and pearl couscous

SERVES 4
PREPARATION 30 minutes
COOKING 3 hours

400 g (14 oz) can whole
    tomatoes
1 small eggplant (aubergine),
    cut into chunks
2 zucchini (courgettes),
    cut into chunks
1 small red capsicum
    (pepper), cut into large
    chunks
1 small green capsicum
    (pepper), cut into large
    chunks
3 cloves garlic, smashed
½ teaspoon dried oregano
2 bay leaves
1 tablespoon extra virgin
    olive oil
1 tablespoon red wine vinegar
½ cup (100 g) pearl or Israeli
    couscous
4 white fish fillets, about
    150–175 g (5½–6 oz) each,
    skin off and pin-boned
handful flat-leaf parsley
    leaves

This is a pretty good example of how clever your slow cooker can be when it is put through its paces. Here, the vegetables are first slow cooked, keeping in all their goodness, then the couscous is added and simmered until tender in the vegetable juices, and finally the fish is simply steamed on top.

Heat your slow cooker to High.

Tip the can of tomatoes into a colander set over a bowl and leave to drain.

Tumble the eggplant, zucchini and both capsicums into the bowl of the slow cooker. Scatter in the garlic, oregano and bay leaves. Tip in the drained tomatoes and pour in 2 tablespoons of the tomato juice from the bowl. Season generously with salt and pepper, then drizzle with the olive oil and vinegar. Cover and cook for 2 hours.

Give the ratatouille a stir, then quickly cover again and cook for a further 30 minutes, until the vegetables are tender.

Working quickly to avoid losing too much heat, stir in the couscous, then lay the fish fillets on top. Cover and cook for 30 minutes, until the couscous is tender and the fish is white and cooked through.

Use a slotted spoon to transfer everything to plates. Spoon some of the sauce over the top and scatter with the parsley leaves.

Polenta with mushrooms, chilli and parmesan

As if by magic, an impossibly wet-looking polenta mixture turns fluffy and pudding-like. If you're feeling extra-posh, there's the option of adding truffle oil, but it is perfectly delicious without. As for the mushrooms, they are beautifully succulent and juicy when steamed in your slow cooker.

SERVES 4
PREPARATION 25 minutes
COOKING 2½ hours

2 cups (380 g) fine polenta
6 cups (1.5 litres) vegetable stock
3 tablespoons extra virgin olive oil
1 teaspoon truffle oil (optional)
1 cup (100 g) finely grated parmesan
3 cups (270 g) small Swiss brown mushrooms
8 shiitake mushrooms
3 cups (270 g) small button mushrooms
3 cloves garlic, finely chopped
½ teaspoon fennel seeds, coarsely crushed
handful finely chopped flat-leaf parsley
1 large red chilli, seeded and finely chopped

● VEGETARIAN
● GLUTEN-FREE

Heat your slow cooker to High.

Put the polenta, stock, truffle oil (if using), 1 tablespoon of the olive oil and 2 tablespoons of the parmesan into the bowl of the slow cooker. Stir with a whisk or wooden spoon, making sure the polenta is thoroughly mixed into the stock and is lump-free. Cover and cook for 1½ hours, until the polenta has absorbed the liquid and is firm but still slightly wobbly.

Towards the end of the cooking time, put all the mushrooms into a large bowl. Add the garlic, fennel seeds, parsley and chilli, along with the remaining 2 tablespoons of olive oil and a generous seasoning of salt and pepper. Toss everything together so the mushrooms are well coated.

Working quickly to avoid losing too much heat, tumble the mushrooms over the polenta. Cover and cook for 1 hour, until the mushrooms have collapsed and are tender and juicy.

Serve with the remaining parmesan on the side.

Pork and veal meatballs with casarecce

SERVES 4
PREPARATION 40 minutes
COOKING 3½ hours

2 x 400 g (14 oz) cans
  crushed tomatoes
3 tablespoons tomato paste
  (concentrated purée)
1 tablespoon cornflour
1 cup (250 ml) chicken stock
½ teaspoon chilli flakes
2 tablespoons extra virgin
  olive oil
1 cup (100 g) casarecce
  pasta
50 g (1¾ oz) parmesan,
  finely shaved
large handful baby rocket
  (arugula), to serve

MEATBALLS
750 g (1 lb 10 oz) pork and
  veal mince
2 cloves garlic, crushed
½ cup (30 g) fresh wholemeal
  breadcrumbs
1 teaspoon fennel seeds,
  crushed
1 teaspoon dried oregano
2 tablespoons finely grated
  parmesan

I really like cooking pasta in the slow cooker. You don't need a large quantity, just a cup or so of a small- or medium-sized pasta; if you want to use long pasta such as spaghetti, you'll need to break it up into smaller pieces. The meatballs can be made in advance and will happily sit in the fridge, ready to be added to a simple tomato sauce for this casual yet satisfying dinner.

First make the meatballs. Combine the mince, garlic, breadcrumbs, fennel seeds, oregano and parmesan in a bowl. Season with salt and pepper, then use your hands to squeeze the mixture until it is well combined. Wet your hands with cold water and roll the mixture into small balls about the size of a walnut, then put on a tray and refrigerate until needed.

Heat your slow cooker to High.

Put the crushed tomatoes, tomato paste, cornflour, stock, chilli flakes and 1 tablespoon of the olive oil into the bowl of the slow cooker. Season generously with salt and pepper, then give everything a good stir. Cover and cook for 2½ hours, until the sauce is bubbling around the edges.

Towards the end of the cooking time, cook the pasta in boiling water for 5 minutes, then drain well.

Working quickly to avoid losing too much heat, give the tomato sauce a quick stir, then add the meatballs, nudging them into the sauce. Tip in the pasta and stir gently, being careful not to break up the meatballs but making sure the pasta is covered in the sauce. Cover and cook for 1 hour, until the pasta is tender and the meatballs are cooked.

Drizzle with the remaining olive oil, scatter with parmesan shavings and serve in bowls, with some rocket on the side.

Steamed salmon with lemony potatoes and broccoli

SERVES 4
PREPARATION 20 minutes
COOKING 3½ hours

8 baby potatoes, cut in half
1 small head broccoli, broken
    into large florets
1 clove garlic, crushed
½ teaspoon chilli flakes
1 tablespoon extra virgin
    olive oil
1 tablespoon chicken stock
1 tablespoon lemon juice
2 tablespoons tarragon
    leaves
handful finely chopped
    flat-leaf parsley
600 g (1 lb 5 oz) salmon fillet,
    skin on
handful roughly chopped dill
lemon wedges, to serve

● **GLUTEN-FREE**

This recipe follows a foolproof formula: tumble vegetables and your chosen flavourings and seasonings into a slow cooker, cook until tender, then lay some fish on top and leave to steam gently. Dinner is served! Here I've gone for a large salmon fillet and broken it into large chunks to serve. You could also use ocean trout fillet, either in one piece or as four portions.

Heat your slow cooker to High.

Tumble the potatoes and broccoli into the bowl of the slow cooker. In a small bowl or jug, combine the garlic, chilli flakes, olive oil, stock, lemon juice, tarragon and parsley. Season generously with salt and pepper, then drizzle all over the vegetables. Cover and cook for 3 hours, until the potatoes are tender when pierced with a fork or skewer.

Working quickly to avoid losing too much heat, lay the salmon, skin side down, on the vegetables. Cover again and cook for 30 minutes, until the salmon flakes easily with a fork.

Remove the fish to a chopping board. Arrange the vegetables on serving plates, then break the salmon into large chunks and place on the plates. Spoon over some of the cooking juices and scatter with the dill. Serve with lemon wedges.

Japanese vegetable and tofu hotpot with udon noodles

SERVES 4
PREPARATION 30 minutes
COOKING 4½ hours

4 cups (1 litre) fish stock
¼ cup (60 ml) tamari
1 tablespoon dashi powder
1 tablespoon mirin
3 cm (1¼ in) piece ginger, thinly sliced
1 cup (40 g) sliced dried shiitake mushrooms
400 g (14 oz) pumpkin, skin on, cut into 2–3 cm (¾–1¼ in) pieces
400 g (14 oz) daikon (white radish), peeled and cut into 2 cm (¾ in) cubes
300 g (10½ oz) firm tofu, cut into cubes
200 g (7 oz) fresh shiitake mushrooms
200 g (7 oz) fresh udon noodles

Authentic Japanese flavours are not as rarefied as you might think, and many of them can be easily picked up at your local supermarket. Dashi is the base flavour behind all those tasty Japanese soups we love – and although it can be complicated to make from scratch, it is conveniently sold in powder form, in little sachets ready to throw into your slow cooker.

Heat your slow cooker to High.

Put the stock, tamari, dashi powder, mirin, ginger and dried mushrooms into the bowl of the slow cooker and stir well. Cover and cook for 2 hours, until the mushrooms are soft.

Add the pumpkin, daikon and tofu, then cover and cook for 2 hours, until the vegetables are tender. Stir through the fresh mushrooms and cover while you prepare the noodles.

Put the noodles into a colander and pour boiling water over them, shaking the colander to dry and separate the noodles. Tip the noodles into the slow cooker, then cover and cook for 30 minutes, until they are cooked through.

Use a slotted spoon to divide the vegetables, tofu and noodles between four bowls. Ladle over some of the stock and sprinkle with freshly ground black pepper to serve.

Chicken tagine with thyme, orange and green olives

SERVES 4
PREPARATION 20 minutes
COOKING about 3 hours

400 g (14 oz) can crushed
   tomatoes
1 cup (250 ml) tomato
   passata (puréed tomatoes)
1 tablespoon olive oil
1 teaspoon thyme leaves
1 teaspoon ground ginger
1 teaspoon ground cumin
1 teaspoon ground coriander
1 teaspoon sweet paprika
1½ cups (375 ml) chicken
   stock
1 tablespoon cornflour
2 oranges
8 chicken tenderloins
12 large green olives
couscous, to serve
dill sprigs, to serve
handful flat-leaf parsley,
   to serve

'Tagine' is the name of both the classic North African dish and the conical-shaped vessel traditionally used to cook it. I love tagines because they disregard the rules: the meat isn't browned off, as it is in classical French or Italian cookery. The meat and all the spices are simply thrown into a pot with liquid and cooked for a long time over a low heat. Which makes me wonder – are slow cookers effectively electric tagines?

Heat your slow cooker to High.

Put the tomatoes, tomato passata, olive oil, thyme, ginger, cumin, coriander, paprika, stock, cornflour and a good seasoning of salt and pepper into the bowl of the slow cooker, stirring to dissolve the cornflour. Peel three thick strips of zest from one of the oranges and stir into the sauce. Cover and cook for 2 hours, until the sauce is bubbling around the edges and the flavours have developed.

Add the chicken and olives, nudging the chicken into the sauce so it is submerged. Cover and cook for 45–60 minutes, until the chicken is white and cooked through.

Meanwhile, peel both of the oranges, removing as much of the pith as possible. Cut between each segment to separate them.

When the chicken is cooked, tumble in the orange segments and leave for 10 minutes to gently warm through in the sauce.

Serve the tagine on a bed of couscous, scattered with the dill and parsley.

Cabbage stuffed with veal, barley and currants

SERVES 4
PREPARATION 45 minutes
COOKING about 4 hours

¼ cup (50 g) pearl barley
1 whole red cabbage
750 g (1 lb 10 oz) veal mince
2 tablespoons currants
½ teaspoon chilli flakes
½ teaspoon dried oregano
small handful finely
    chopped dill
small handful finely chopped
    flat-leaf parsley
3 cups (750 ml) tomato
    passata (puréed tomatoes)
400 g (14 oz) can crushed
    tomatoes
1 tablespoon extra virgin
    olive oil
handful dill sprigs, to serve

You will need a whole cabbage to give you cabbage leaves large enough for stuffing. If you want to get a head start, you could stuff the cabbage leaves in the morning, or even the day before, and pop them in the fridge. Then all that's left to do is the sauce.

Cook the barley in a small saucepan of boiling water for 15 minutes, to slightly soften. Drain well and set aside.

Cut off the stem of the cabbage and discard. Put the cabbage in a large heatproof bowl and pour in enough boiling water to submerge it. Leave for about 10 minutes for the leaves to soften, using tongs to turn the cabbage a couple of times. Transfer to a chopping board, and when the cabbage is cool enough to handle, peel off the thick, outer leaves and use two or three of them to line the bowl of the slow cooker.

Carefully remove the softer inner leaves, keeping them intact, until you have eight reasonably sized ones. Cut out the hard, white central core and discard, then set the leaves aside.

In a bowl, combine the mince, currants, chilli flakes, oregano, dill and parsley with the barley and a generous seasoning of salt and pepper. Use your hands to combine thoroughly.

Heat your slow cooker to High.

Lay the cabbage leaves on a work surface with the stem end facing you. Put one-eighth of the filling in the centre of each leaf, then fold over, tucking in the sides, to enclose the filling. Arrange the stuffed cabbage leaves so they fit snugly side-by-side in your slow cooker. Pour in the passata and tomatoes and season generously with salt and pepper. Drizzle with the olive oil, then cover and cook for 3 hours.

Working quickly to avoid losing too much heat, gently separate the cabbage rolls to allow the sauce to seep in between them. Cover and cook for a further 30 minutes, then transfer to serving plates and garnish with dill sprigs.

Osso buco with Mediterranean vegetables

SERVES 4
PREPARATION 30 minutes
COOKING 3½ hours

4 slices osso buco, about
    200 g (7 oz) each
400 g (14 oz) can crushed
    tomatoes
¼ cup (60 ml) beef stock
2 tablespoons cornflour
pinch saffron strands
1 teaspoon dried oregano
1 bay leaf
2 cloves garlic, crushed
handful finely chopped
    flat-leaf parsley
1 red capsicum (pepper),
    sliced
2 small zucchini (courgettes),
    cut into thick rounds
1 small eggplant (aubergine),
    cut into large bite-sized
    chunks
1 tablespoon finely grated
    lemon zest
finely grated parmesan,
    to serve

● GLUTEN-FREE

Literally meaning 'hole in the bone', osso buco is the name used for the cut of meat that is a cross-section slice of veal shin. You don't want giant dinner-plate-sized slices, though, as these may be from older cows and can be tough. Look for slices no bigger than a saucer – these are from younger calves and will be leaner. With fall-apart tender meat and colourful vegetables, this osso buco is sensational served on a bed of mashed sweet potato.

Heat your slow cooker to High.

Trim off all the fat from the osso buco and discard. Refrigerate the meat until needed.

Put the tomatoes, stock, cornflour, saffron, oregano, bay leaf, garlic and most of the parsley (reserving a little to sprinkle over the finished dish) into the bowl of the slow cooker. Season generously with salt and pepper, then give everything a good stir, making sure the cornflour has dissolved. Stir in the capsicum, zucchini and eggplant.

Lay the osso buco on top and nudge it into the vegetable mixture so it is just slightly covered by some of the sauce. Cover and cook for 3 hours, until the sauce is bubbling around the edges.

Give it a stir, then quickly cover again to avoid losing too much heat. Cook for a further 30 minutes, until the meat and vegetables are tender.

Transfer to serving bowls and sprinkle with the remaining parsley, lemon zest and parmesan.

Beef, freekeh and leek stew

SERVES 4
PREPARATION 20 minutes
COOKING 3 hours

1 large leek, white part only
500 g (1 lb 2 oz) chuck steak
1 tablespoon cornflour
250 g (9 oz) fresh shiitake
    mushrooms, halved
½ cup (20 g) chopped dried
    porcini mushrooms
4 sprigs thyme
2 cloves garlic, finely chopped
1 large tomato, roughly
    chopped
½ cup (100 g) whole freekeh
1½ cups (375 ml) beef stock
1 tablespoon dark soy sauce
handful finely chopped
    flat-leaf parsley

The fire-roasted green grains of wheat called freekeh are nutty and a little bit smoky, adding both taste and texture to this hearty stew. Dried and fresh mushrooms, along with dark soy sauce, give a rich chestnut colour and a deep savoury flavour.

Heat your slow cooker to High.

Cut the leek in half lengthways, then cut into thick ribbons. Scatter half of the leeks into the bowl of the slow cooker.

Trim off all the fat from the beef and discard. Cut the meat into 4–5 cm (1½–2 in) chunks and put into a bowl. Add the cornflour, tossing to coat the beef all over.

Sit the beef on top of the leeks, then scatter in the fresh and dried mushrooms, thyme, garlic, tomato and freekeh. Season generously with salt and pepper. Pour in the stock and soy sauce, then cover and cook for 2 hours.

Give everything a good stir, then quickly cover again to avoid losing too much heat. Cook for 1 hour, until the beef is tender.

Serve in bowls, scattered with the parsley.

Mushroom ragu with spaghetti

SERVES 4
PREPARATION 20 minutes
COOKING about 2½ hours

1 tablespoon olive oil
1 brown onion, finely chopped
2 cloves garlic, finely chopped
400 g (14 oz) can crushed tomatoes
2 tablespoons tomato paste (concentrated purée)
2 teaspoons vegetable stock powder
2 teaspoons cornflour
2 teaspoons dark soy sauce
small handful tarragon leaves
large handful finely chopped flat-leaf parsley
2 cups (180 g) small button mushrooms
2 cups (180 g) quartered Swiss brown mushrooms
¼ cup (10 g) chopped dried porcini mushrooms
½ cup (125 g) light sour cream
300 g (10½ oz) wholemeal spaghetti
½ cup (50 g) finely grated parmesan, to serve

● VEGETARIAN

Mushrooms can be partnered with pretty much the same ingredients as beef: tomatoes, red wine and strong-flavoured herbs spring to mind. I would probably avoid more delicate mushroom varieties like oyster and enoki here, as they won't benefit from slow cooking as much as the more robust button mushrooms and Swiss browns. For a gluten-free meal, simply serve with some mashed potato or polenta instead of the pasta.

Heat your slow cooker to High.

Put the olive oil into a large frying pan over high heat. When the oil is hot, add the onion and garlic and fry for a couple of minutes. Remove from the heat and stir in the tomatoes, tomato paste, stock powder, cornflour, soy sauce, tarragon, most of the parsley (reserving a little to scatter over the finished dish) and ¼ cup (60 ml) water. Season generously with salt and pepper, then tip the lot into the bowl of the slow cooker.

Add the mushrooms and give everything a good stir. Cover and cook for 2 hours, until the mushrooms are tender and the sauce is thick and rich.

Working quickly to avoid losing too much heat, stir through the sour cream. Cover and cook for a further 30 minutes.

Towards the end of the cooking time, cook the spaghetti in boiling water according to the packet instructions. Drain well.

Serve the mushroom ragu with the spaghetti, scattered with the parmesan and the reserved parsley.

Sicilian tuna with tomato, currants and pine nuts

SERVES 4
PREPARATION 15 minutes
COOKING about 2½ hours

2 tablespoons olive oil
1 small red onion, thinly sliced
2 cloves garlic, finely chopped
¼ cup (40 g) pine nuts
2 tablespoons currants
6 sprigs thyme
400 g (14 oz) can cherry
    tomatoes
½ cup (125 ml) vegetable
    stock
4 tuna steaks, each about
    150–175 g (5½–6 oz)
handful finely chopped
    flat-leaf parsley
orange wedges, to serve

● GLUTEN-FREE

The flavours here evoke the sunny disposition of southern Italy, where sweet currants, pine nuts and citrus are commonly used when cooking seafood. Tuna can be a bit pricey, but it makes for a real weekend treat. If you can't find good tuna steaks, firm white fish fillets or mackerel would do very nicely.

Heat your slow cooker to High.

Put 1 tablespoon of the olive oil into a frying pan over medium heat. When the oil is hot, add the onion, garlic and pine nuts and fry for a few minutes, until the onion is soft and the pine nuts are turning golden. Remove from the heat and stir through the currants, thyme, tomatoes and stock. Season generously with salt, then tip the lot into the bowl of the slow cooker. Give everything a good stir, then cover and cook for 2 hours, until the sauce is thick and rich.

Season the tuna steaks with salt and pepper. Lay the tuna fillets on top of the tomato mixture in the slow cooker. Drizzle in the remaining olive oil, then cover and cook for a further 30 minutes, until the tuna is just cooked through.

Serve with the parsley scattered over and the orange wedges on the side for squeezing.

Pumpkin and chickpea tagine with red onion and fresh herbs

SERVES 4
PREPARATION 25 minutes
COOKING 3 hours

400 g (14 oz) jap pumpkin, skin on, cut into wedges
400 g (14 oz) can chickpeas, rinsed and well drained
3 cloves garlic, finely chopped
3 cm (1¼ in) piece ginger, finely chopped
1 large red chilli, thinly sliced
2 teaspoons ground cumin
2 teaspoons hot paprika
2 tablespoons olive oil
1 tablespoon finely chopped preserved lemon
1 cup (250 ml) vegetable stock
1 small red onion, thinly sliced
handful flat-leaf parsley leaves
handful coriander (cilantro) leaves
handful mint leaves

● VEGAN
● GLUTEN-FREE

Pumpkin is something you have to watch out for in a slow cooker, because it takes much longer to cook than you might think, especially if there's only a little liquid. This gorgeous golden-hued tagine is just fine on its own, but if you want to push the boat out, tumble some raw prawns on top for the last 30 minutes of cooking.

Heat your slow cooker to High.

Put the pumpkin, chickpeas, garlic, ginger, chilli, cumin, paprika, olive oil and preserved lemon into a large bowl. Season generously with salt and pepper, toss to combine thoroughly, then tumble into the bowl of the slow cooker. Pour in the stock, cover and cook for 3 hours, until the pumpkin is very tender.

Transfer the pumpkin and chickpea tagine to a large platter. Combine the red onion and herbs in a bowl, then scatter over the tagine.

Prawn saganaki

SERVES 4
PREPARATION 20 minutes
COOKING 2½ hours

2 tablespoons extra virgin
    olive oil
1 red onion, thinly sliced
2 cloves garlic, finely chopped
2 cloves
1 teaspoon dried oregano
¼ teaspoon ground mace
    or nutmeg
400 g (14 oz) can crushed
    tomatoes
1 tablespoon tomato paste
    (concentrated purée)
½ cup (125 ml) vegetable
    stock
24 raw prawns, peeled and
    deveined, but with tails
    intact
200 g (7 oz) Greek feta,
    roughly crumbled
handful finely chopped
    flat-leaf parsley
handful finely chopped dill
lemon wedges, to serve

● GLUTEN-FREE

In Greek cookery, saganaki generally refers to any dish with cheese that's made in a small frying pan. A slow cooker may not exactly be a pan, but this works just as well, if not better – during the long, slow cooking, the feta softens to a soufflé-like texture.

Heat your slow cooker to High.

Put 1 tablespoon of the olive oil in a frying pan over high heat. Add the onion and garlic and fry for about 5 minutes, until the onion has softened. Add the cloves, oregano and mace, then remove from the heat. Stir in the crushed tomatoes, tomato paste, stock and a generous seasoning of salt and pepper.

Tip the lot into the bowl of the slow cooker and cook for 2 hours, until the sauce is bubbling and aromatic.

Scatter the prawns over the sauce, spreading them out so they don't overlap. Drizzle with the remaining olive oil and season with salt and pepper. Scatter in the feta, parsley and dill, then cover and cook for 30 minutes, until the prawns are pink and cooked through.

Serve in bowls, with lemon wedges on the side.

Chicken with pomegranate molasses, prunes and potatoes

SERVES 4
PREPARATION 25 minutes
COOKING 3 hours

8 chicken thigh fillets
1 tablespoon olive oil
2 large brown onions, cut
    into thin wedges
2 teaspoons ground cumin
1 teaspoon ground cinnamon
1 teaspoon ground ginger
1 teaspoon ras el hanout
1½ cups (375 ml) chicken
    stock
1 tablespoon cornflour
1 tablespoon pomegranate
    molasses
pinch saffron strands
6 small waxy potatoes,
    skin on, halved
12 pitted prunes
handful flat-leaf parsley,
    finely chopped
large handful mint leaves

● GLUTEN-FREE

With two or three hours of cooking, chicken thighs are rendered melt-in-your-mouth tender. Because of this lengthy cooking time, I always use a firm potato variety here, as floury potatoes would just fall apart. If you are super-organised, you could make this luscious chicken casserole the day before and refrigerate it, then reheat just before serving; the flavours will only improve with an overnight rest.

Trim all the fat from the chicken and discard. Cut each thigh in half and refrigerate until needed.

Heat your slow cooker to High.

Put the olive oil into a frying pan over high heat. When the oil is hot, add the onion and fry for about 5 minutes, until soft and golden. Stir through the cumin, cinnamon, ginger and ras el hanout and season generously with salt and pepper. Remove from the heat.

Put the stock, cornflour, pomegranate molasses and saffron into the bowl of the slow cooker, stirring to dissolve the cornflour. Scrape in the contents of the frying pan and stir to combine, then add the chicken, potatoes, prunes and parsley. Mix thoroughly, then cover and cook for 2 hours.

Give everything a good stir, then quickly cover again to avoid losing too much heat. Cook for 1 hour, until the chicken is cooked through and the sauce is thick and fragrant.

Serve with mint leaves on the side to tear up and scatter over.

Mediterranean seafood and couscous stew

SERVES 4
PREPARATION 20 minutes
COOKING about 3 hours

2 tablespoons extra virgin olive oil
1 large red onion, finely chopped
2 cloves garlic, crushed
½ teaspoon fennel seeds
½ teaspoon chilli flakes
400 g (14 oz) can crushed tomatoes
1 cup (250 ml) seafood stock
3 strips lemon zest
¼ cup (50 g) instant couscous
12 large raw prawns, peeled and deveined, but with tails intact
16 ready-to-cook black mussels
300 g (10½ oz) squid hoods, cut into rings

Couscous is used here to thicken the stew and bring everything together; it doesn't become gloopy and stodgy, but stays slightly crunchy and nutty. If you wanted to get ahead, you could make the tomato sauce in advance, cooking it for the required time and then refrigerating it until needed. About half an hour before you want to eat, just reheat the sauce on High in your slow cooker and when it is bubbling around the edges, throw in the couscous and seafood and proceed.

Heat your slow cooker to High.

Heat the olive oil in a frying pan over medium heat. Add the onion, garlic, fennel seeds and chilli flakes and when they start to sizzle in the oil, give them a good stir and remove from the heat.

Put the tomatoes, stock and lemon zest into the bowl of the slow cooker. Tip in the contents of the frying pan and season generously with salt and pepper, then give everything a good stir. Cover and cook for 2½ hours, until the flavours have developed and the sauce is bubbling around the edges.

Working quickly to avoid losing too much heat, stir through the couscous, followed by the prawns, mussels and squid. Cover and cook for 20–30 minutes, until all the seafood is cooked and the couscous has absorbed much of the liquid.

Transfer to a large serving dish.

Buddha's delight

SERVES 4
PREPARATION 20 minutes
COOKING 2½ hours

1 cup (250 ml) vegetable
   stock
1 tablespoon light soy sauce
2 tablespoons cornflour
2 teaspoons sesame oil
125 g (4½ oz) baby corn,
   cut in half
225 g (8 oz) can sliced
   bamboo shoots, drained
12 fresh shiitake mushrooms,
   cut in half
12 Swiss brown mushrooms
6 oyster mushrooms, torn
   in half
5 cm (2 in) piece ginger,
   thinly sliced
300 g (10½ oz) marinated
   tofu, sliced
1 bunch Chinese broccoli,
   cut into 5–6 cm
   (2–2½ in) lengths

● VEGAN

This well-known Chinese Buddhist dish is indeed delightful, and is guaranteed to lift the spirits. Note that this recipe lacks garlic, the pungent flavour of which apparently has the potential to excite and arouse, interfering with clarity of mind and intent.

Heat your slow cooker to High.

Put the stock, soy sauce, cornflour and half of the sesame oil into the bowl of the slow cooker. Season generously with salt and pepper, then give everything a good stir to dissolve the cornflour. Stir in the corn, bamboo shoots, mushrooms, ginger and tofu. Cover and cook for 1½ hours.

Working quickly to avoid losing too much heat, tumble in the Chinese broccoli. Cover and cook for 1 hour, until it is steamed and tender.

Drizzle with the remaining sesame oil and transfer to a large serving bowl or serve directly from the slow cooker.

Fava beans with green beans, mint and feta

SERVES 4
PREPARATION 20 minutes
COOKING 2½ hours

850 g (1 lb 14 oz) can fava
    beans
400 g (14 oz) can diced
    tomatoes
½ cup (90 g) sliced roasted
    red capsicum (pepper)
1 large red onion, finely
    chopped
1 teaspoon ground cumin
handful finely chopped
    flat-leaf parsley
handful finely chopped dill
2 tablespoons olive oil
150 g (5½ oz) green beans,
    trimmed
50 g (1¾ oz) feta, crumbled
handful mint leaves

● VEGETARIAN
● GLUTEN-FREE

When reconstituted and cooked, dried broad beans – often called fava beans – are rich and meaty, quite different from vivid-green fresh broad beans . I'm going to go out on a limb here and say that I prefer them. And, even better, you can get them all ready to go in a can. The green beans are tumbled on top and steamed to a crispy goodness.

Heat your slow cooker to High.

Put the fava beans into a colander and rinse under the cold tap, using your hands to separate any that are stuck together. Drain well and tip into the bowl of the slow cooker.

Add the tomatoes, capsicum, onion, cumin, parsley, dill and 1 tablespoon of the olive oil. Season generously with salt and pepper, then give everything a good stir. Cover and cook for 2 hours, until the beans are very tender and the sauce has thickened.

Working quickly to avoid losing too much heat, scatter in the green beans and drizzle with the remaining olive oil. Cover and cook for 30 minutes until the beans are steamed and crisp.

Serve in bowls, scattered with crumbled feta and garnished with mint leaves.

Mexican prawns with coriander rice

SERVES 4
PREPARATION 20 minutes
COOKING 2½ hours

400 g (14 oz) can whole
    tomatoes
2 tablespoons chipotle sauce
1 white onion, roughly
    chopped
2 cloves garlic, roughly
    chopped
large handful roughly
    chopped coriander
    (cilantro)
2 tablespoons lime juice
1½ cups (300 g) long-grain
    rice
12 large raw prawns, peeled
    and deveined, but with
    tails intact
handful baby spinach leaves
handful coriander (cilantro)
    leaves, to serve
lime wedges, to serve

● GLUTEN-FREE

Your slow cooker makes really good steamed rice, as it works in much the same way as a rice cooker. Just make sure you give the rice a thorough rinse beforehand. Once the rice is cooked, you can top it with light ingredients; nothing too heavy, or the rice will turn into a stodgy mess. Try this zesty, tomato-based sauce with prawns (or fillets of white fish, if you prefer). I tend to avoid adding frozen seafood directly to the slow cooker, as it releases too much water. If you are using frozen prawns, make sure they are completely thawed and pat dry with paper towel.

Heat your slow cooker to High.

Put the tomatoes, chipotle sauce, onion, garlic, coriander and lime juice into a food processor and process until you have a smooth sauce. Tip into a large bowl and set aside.

Rinse the rice in a fine sieve under the cold tap until the water runs clear. Drain well, then tip into the bowl of the slow cooker. Add 2 cups (500 ml) water, cover and cook for 1½ hours, until almost all the liquid has been absorbed.

Stir the prawns into the bowl of tomato sauce, then gently pour over the rice in the slow cooker, spreading the prawns out so they don't overlap. Cover and cook for 1 hour, until they are pink and cooked through.

Serve in bowls with baby spinach and coriander leaves on the side, and lime wedges for squeezing.

Acknowledgements

It's always a team effort making a book such as this.

Thank you, Jane Morrow. It was serendipity that I ran into Jane in the corridors of Murdoch Books, and she then offered me this project. On that note, thanks heaps to all the crew at Murdoch Books who pulled this one together: Jane Price, Sarah Odgers and Megan Pigott. Also a big hug to my old mate, Alison Cowan – it's been lovely to reconnect with her doing this book.

I would not have made it through the massive task of recipe testing without my darling sister, Susie, and her very hungry family. They were my best critics, and it meant that nothing went to waste! I'm blessed that my sister lives just around the corner.

On to the photography: we could not have had a better team, and I think it shows. Stylist Vanessa Austin yet again brought her wand to weave her magic – Vanessa is akin to the good witch in the Wizard of Oz! Jeremy Simons, photographer, is the loveliest bloke you could meet, and takes beautiful pictures to boot. (He also has one very cute dog, Chef. Woof!) And, thank you, to my newly found friend, Meryl Butterworth, a gorgeous and talented soul who is also a whiz in the kitchen.

What a team! Thank you.

Index

Published in 2019 by Murdoch Books, an imprint of Allen & Unwin

Murdoch Books Australia
83 Alexander Street, Crows Nest
NSW 2065
Phone: +61 (0)2 8425 0100
murdochbooks.com.au
info@murdochbooks.com.au

Murdoch Books UK
Ormond House, 26–27 Boswell Street,
London, WC1N 3JZ
Phone: +44 (0) 20 8785 5995
murdochbooks.co.uk
info@murdochbooks.co.uk

For corporate orders & custom publishing contact our business development
team at salesenquiries@murdochbooks.com.au

Publisher: Jane Morrow
Editorial Manager: Jane Price
Design Manager: Megan Pigott
Editor: Alison Cowan
Designer: Sarah Odgers
Photography: Jeremy Simons
Food Preparation for Photography: Meryl Butterworth, Peta Dent
Stylist: Vanessa Austin
Production Director: Lou Playfair

ISBN 978 1 76052 429 6 Australia
ISBN 978 1 91163 220 7 UK

A cataloguing-in-publication entry is available from the catalogue of the
National Library of Australia at nla.gov.au
A catalogue record for this book is available from the British Library

Colour reproduction by Splitting Image Colour Studio Pty Ltd, Clayton, Victoria
Printed by C&C Offset Printing Co Ltd, China

TABLESPOON MEASURES: We have used Australian 20 ml (4 teaspoon)
tablespoon measures. If you are using a smaller European 15 ml (3 teaspoon)
tablespoon, add an extra teaspoon of the ingredient for each tablespoon specified.